More Memories

of

Glasgow

The publishers would like to thank the following companies for their

support in the production of this book

Main Sponsor

Hutchesons' Grammar School

Annan Gallery

Behar Carpets and Flooring

CRGP and Allied Surveyors Scotland Plc

Corston Sinclair Limited

Jonathan Harvey Limited

Morrison Bowmore Distillers Limited

Smith of Whiteinch

WG Spowart Limited

First published in Great Britain by True North Books Limited
England HX5 9AE
01422 377977

ISBN 1 903204 44 5

Text, design and origination by True North Books Limited
Printed and bound by The Amadeus Press Limited

More Memories of Glasgow

Contents

Introduction

The world in which we live is changing daily, making it increasingly difficult to recall with any accuracy what went before. It is easy for our minds to play tricks upon us as we try to conjure up recollections of people and places of yesteryear. That is where the camera and books, such as 'More Memories of Glasgow', can help bring back to life the times we and our parents have lived through. Inside these pages is a feast of images of our city as it has developed over the last 75 years, all pointed up with meaningful text that will help readers, both young and old, to turn back the clock to the days when tramcars clanked their way through Anderston and Cowcaddens. There are memories of the great days of shipbuilding on the Clyde, exhibitions in Bellahouston Park and the sight of baby Austins and Ford Prefects chugging along Buchanan Street. You will be returned to the days when shops had their own individuality, rather than being swallowed up inside a giant shopping mall. Waves of nostalgia for those 20th century moments will come flooding back as readers are

taken back as though on board some modern Tardis or on a journey as in 'Back to the Future'. Perhaps this book will help settle a few arguments about McColl's fruiterers at the Botanic Gardens, Kay Street baths or dancing the quickstep at the Locarno to the sound of the Benny Daniels Orchestra. Whatever your memories of our famous city might be, they will be sharpened by turning the pages of a book that has so much to offer as a window to the past.

Not everything you will come across is guaranteed to evoke happy memories, for we have experienced trauma along the way. Some of our major industries went into decline, there was overcrowding and cramped conditions for those living in the inner city and the privations of wartime to be endured. These are the crosses many Glaswegians had to bear, so it would be inaccurate to ignore them, for without recognising the pain how can we fully rejoice in the great pleasures living in our noble city have brought us? We learn as much from the mistakes of the past as we do from its successes, but it is with the latter that

A bustling Sauchiehall Street in 1949.

we can take the greatest heart. As we look to the future that nostalgia for the past is merely something upon which we can build. Even so, there is nothing wrong in allowing a little self indulgence, for the world would be a sadder place if we could not smile with affection as cherished moments come racing back as we enjoy 'More Memories of Glasgow'.

Scotland's second largest city has come a long way from the days when St Kentigern, or St Mungo, built his church in 543 AD on the spot where Glasgow Cathedral now stands. The city's founder performed four miracles, all commemorated in the coat of arms. The tree is a symbol of the lighted branch that illuminated the monastery in Culross, the salmon and ring recall the finding of the lost ring of the Queen of Cadzow, the bell tolled a call to prayer and the robin was the bird that St Kentigern brought back to life. But, perhaps the greatest miracle is the one that Glasgow's inhabitants have continually performed ever since, turning a small religious community into Scotland's largest city. As it grew, taking on the name that is Celtic for 'green glen' or 'dear green place', Glasgow was designated a burgh of barony by William the Conqueror and

about 1189 was granted the right to hold an annual fair. The first stone bridge over the Clyde was built in 1350 and Glasgow was created a royal burgh in 1450, its university being founded the following year. Glasgow prospered as a market centre because it was well situated between Highland and Lowland Scotland and also between Edinburgh and the west, but its population was only some 2,000. Yet it was not until after the union of the Scottish and English crowns in 1603 that Glasgow grew significantly, particularly when trade with the Americas developed. By the end of the 18th century 66,000 could claim it as their home. With the Industrial Revolution came coal mining, iron founding, chemical manufacturing and, especially, shipbuilding, which developed in Glasgow early in the 19th century. The prosperity of Glasgow's shipbuilding and heavy industry was badly shaken after World War I and its industry has since tended toward greater variety. From the mid 20th century the notorious slum tenement areas, such as the Gorbals, were given over to high rise redevelopment schemes. Peripheral new towns grew and reduced the inner city's population and congestion. There were over 1,000,000 under

A busy scene in Glasgow Cross in 1933.

the city's administration at the start of World War II, but boundary changes and population drift have brought this figure down to about 616,000 these days.

This brief flip through 1,500 years of history now sets the scene for 'More Memories of Glasgow' as we wallow in the nostalgia of the last century. The way we shopped, how we played, the jobs we had and the manner of transport used to get around will all hold something special for each and every one of us delving into the pages of this book. We are going to return to butchers' shops where hares and poultry hung on hooks outside the premises, newsagents who sold 'Film Fun', 'Picture Post' and the saucy 'Reveille' and hair stylists who gave us the bob, the Toni perm and the Purdy. There were bars of Fry's Five Boys, Mackintosh's Munchies, bullseyes and sherbet dips to enjoy, whilst dad lit up a Woodbine or mum a Kensitas with a Swan Vesta. We rubbed Germolene on chapped legs and drank draughts of Ovaltine, proudly sporting a Robertson's Golly badge on our chests. Men wore suits and ladies went into town wearing a hat, whilst little girls had bobbysox and boys wore short trousers beneath their school

blazers. We had conker and marble seasons in the playground, charged around madly in games of tig and 40 a side soccer and groomed our dollies' hair. There were trams to dodge and ticket rolls to collect, conductors to pay and I-Spy books to be filled in on car journeys. A different language of measure was on our lips as we talked of stones and hundredweights, gallons and gills or tanners and half crowns. All this and more will be brought back to life as the reader recalls how it all was when wage packets were tipped up on the kitchen table and internet was what you did with the fish you had just caught.

So, prepare for the treasures that are on show as you turn the first leaf by winding up the gramophone and putting on an old 78 by Jimmy Shand or Kenneth McKellar. Dance the 'Bluebell Polka', sing along to 'My love is like a red, red rose' or solve the conundrum of exactly where did Andy Stewart's Donald leave his trousers. The answer to that may not be revealed, but what will is a lasting image of the development of a city that has been shaped by developers, prospered under businessmen and has been made what it is today by us, the people of Glasgow.

Street scenes

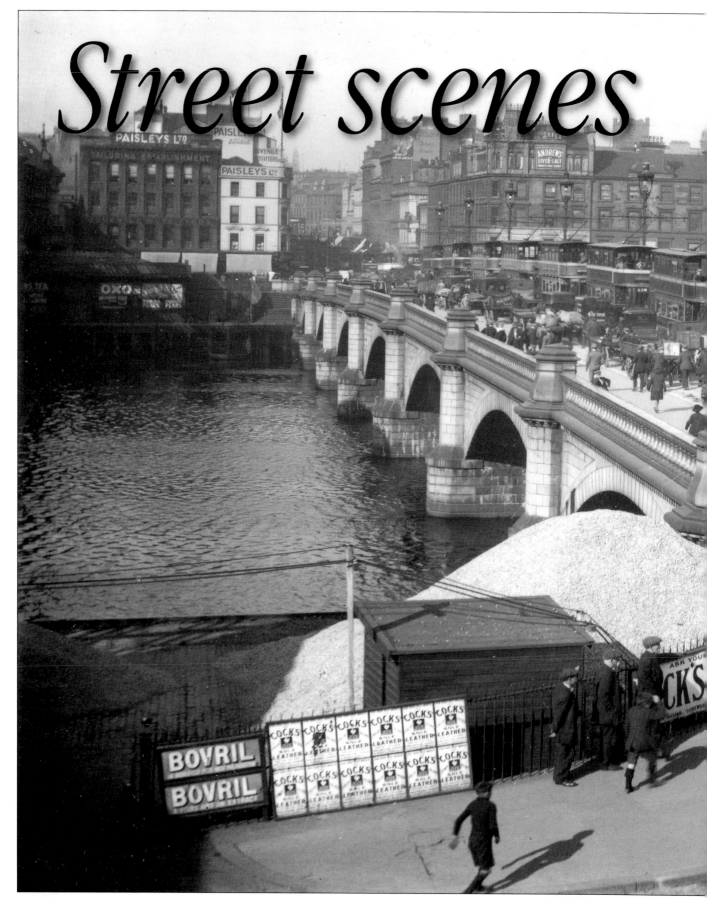

What a lovely mix of old world meeting new was on display on Jamaica Bridge in 1924. There were horse drawn carts and wagons, petrol engined cars and lorries and electrically powered trams all struggling for supremacy. Many of the advertisers on the hoardings and billboards had names that stood the test of time throughout the last century. Oxo, Bovril, Swan Vestas and Pears' soap all flourished, even if the style of promotion changed. Even Lux soap flakes had a long run before being confined to a museum of contemporary history, but it is hard to imagine that Cock's English oak bark leather had quite the same lengthy impact upon the retail world. Jamaica Bridge owes its name to one of Glasgow's sources of prosperity. In the 1700s men, known as the 'tobacco lords', made their fortunes by investing in trade in tobacco with the American colonies. Profits were ploughed into West Indian sugar and cotton growing. Known more often today as Glasgow Bridge, it was built in 1899 by Blyth and Westland, replacing Thomas Telford's structure that in 1835 was, at a width of 60 feet, considered wide enough for even the heaviest traffic. It was a forlorn hope and even the replacement seven arched bridge struggled to cope with the demands put upon it. Broomielaw Bridge, the first one to cross the river at this point, was only half the width of Telford's. Imagine the chaos if that had still been there in 1924!

Queen Street leads north from Argyle Street towards the City Chambers on George Square. Despite the lack of money about in 1946, there were still numbers of shoppers on the pavements and cars on the streets. Petrol had to be carefully eked out as the system of ration coupons meant that only essential motoring was sensible. Some got round the shortages by buying on the black market, but this was not to be recommended as, not only was it illegal, but there were some very unsavoury types involved who would be just as happy to take your money and run as they would be to honour the deal. One third of the way up Queen Street, on the left, is the entrance to South Exchange Court, built in 1830, where there is a plaque to the Victorian poet Alexander Smith who worked in the building as a pattern designer. Queen Street has two particularly interesting buildings at its northern end. The Bank of Scotland, on the corner of St Vincent Place, dates from 1870 and reflects the Victorians' interest in business and good works in the figures of Justice and Plenty that flank the bank's old coat of arms. The main hall is now a pub, but it has kept most of the attractive interior. The Merchants' House Buildings, near Queen Street Station, is an elegant structure acting as a link to the men who helped Glasgow to prosper.

Glasgow has its fair share of long, straight thoroughfares and Renfield Street is no exception. Renfield Street runs mainly from Central station to Renfrew Street and trams once made regular journeys along here to and from Mosspark and Pollokshields. RG Lawrie and Reid & Co were just two of the names readers might recall from retailers plying their trade on Renfield Street, whilst others will have shared many a happy time spent in the Paramount. Renfield and Renfrew have often given rise to confusion because of the similarity of their names and origins. It came about as Campbell of Blythswood's estate, near Renfrew, was called Renfield. He conferred the name of his important Glasgow holding on his residential property, but then proceeded to name two of the new city streets as Renfield and Renfrew respectively. To make matters worse, they adjoin one another and there has been many a heart broken when a girl has been left standing down by the station, whilst her date has fretted away somewhere near Charing Cross! 'Meet you at the end of Renfrew Street' was a message that meant a good five minute walk away, if you misheard and went to Renfield Street. Sometimes it was a good excuse to cover up a late arrival by pretending to have been on time but at the wrong place. However, it was a tale that could only be told once.

Renfield Street changes into Union Street where its southern end meets Gordon Street and it is from this spot that we look further south towards the junction at Argyle Street. The scene on Union Street is typical of around 1950 when cars vied for road space with the greedy trams that hogged the carriageway. They were immovable from their tracks, of course, but that did not stop irate motorists trying to force their way in front of them. The car attempting to turn away from the kerb and join the flow probably had a long wait, because you did not argue with the bulk of the tramcar. In 1950 the Labour government was returned to power in the general election, giving Clement Attlee a second term of office as prime minister. The result was the closest for 100 years, giving the Labour party sleepless nights as its majority of nearly 150 was whittled away to single figures. It seemed as if the general public approved of the Welfare State it created in 1945, but had little time for the lack of decent economic management the government had shown. People seemed little better placed than during the war years, as rationing and austere measures still bit deep, making some query who had been the real victors after all. In February, Scotland said a sad goodbye to Sir Harry Lauder, the loveable little entertainer who was to go roamin' in the gloamin' no more. In October of the following year another general election was held, returning Churchill and the Tories to Downing Street.

ong shadows fell towards Glasgow Cross in 1933 that somehow suggested the gloomy times that people knew. The inter war years were difficult as the days of the depression bit hard with unemployment high and wages low. For many it was a time just to stand around and hope that an upturn would come, although rearmament of the navy stalled the process of decline to some extent as the second world war beckoned. In this year Germany voted in a new Chancellor, someone called Adolf Hitler. We knew little about him, other than he cut a rather silly figure with his foolish moustache and all that arm waving. We were soon to sing a different tune. Glasgow Cross was the area where the first recognised centre of shopping was established and is one of the city's most historic sites, though much of the architecture today is quite modern. It is the meeting place for several important streets and has always been a busy, congested spot. The Tolbooth Steeple, dominating the centre of the picture, dates from 1627 and was part of a larger building that housed the council hall, offices and the gaol. Beneath its seven storeys punishment was meted out to various miscreants whose crimes ranged from murder to petty theft. It was also a spot where rich merchants promenaded with their sumptuously dressed ladies, showing off their worth to the passing hoi-polloi.

Above: Looking along Woodlands Road from the junction with St George's Road on 24 September 1958 it would appear that you are witnessing a convention of tramcars and trolleybuses, with the 'caurs' taking the major role. It was not to be so for much longer because, in 1962, the trams breathed their last, much to the sadness of traditionalists who saw in their demise the passing of an old friend. The end of the trolleybuses in 1967 caused few similar emotions, as they had never attracted the same affection during the 18 years they had been seen on the city streets. Some dubbed them 'silent death' as they were so quiet, gliding along the roads, as compared with noisy buses or trams. It was a familiar site to see a trolleybus stopped in the middle of the road, with the driver attempting to get the trolley bar back on the overhead electric cable using a long insulated pole. It usually provided cheeky little boys who were passing with an opportunity to goad the driver with jokes at his expense. The junction of Woodlands Road at Charing Cross is greatly changed now that exit 18 of the motorway marks the spot, but the rest of the road and its buildings, heading out towards Great Western Road, have largely survived unaltered.

Above: This 1955 bird's eye view of Hope Street helps give us an idea of the grandeur of many of Glasgow's buildings that we miss at street level. It would be a good idea if we took time off from all our other activities just to walk around the city streets, looking upwards. Better still would be to do that with the help of a pair of binoculars, squinting through the lens as we craned our necks to get the best view of the gargoyles, cherubs, cupolas, turrets and carved figures that adorn these testaments to the vision of the architects and the skill of the builders. If you did so, there is a risk of being arrested and whisked off in a straitjacket, but it would be well worth it for the aesthetic pleasures that had been gained. Even a single thoroughfare, such as Hope Street, can boast its own privileged collection of grand, imposing structures. At the top of the street there are McConnel's Building, the old Athenaeum and the Theatre Royal, the home of Scottish opera. The lofty Lion Chambers and the former Pot Still pub are further down, whilst the eight storey office block dominating the corner with West George Street has some interesting art nouveau as well as decorative designs. Passengers travelling on the top deck of the trams got a better sight of these than pedestrians on the pavement, but for a proper appreciation just pass over those 'bins'.

In the past Argyle Street has been called Dumbarton Road, Wester Gate and Anderson Walk, but was given its new name, if not the spelling, in memory of Archibald, Duke of Argyll, one of the first group of Scottish lords to sit at the Parliament of Great Britain. Wearing the full Monty, as a set of clothes bought from Montague Burton's tailor's store was known, the young men on Argyle Street were off to enjoy a night out on the town in 1962. Their clothing of smart suits, slim Jim ties, narrow shoes and tight trousers would undergo fundamental changes as the decade progressed. For generations men dressed themselves and groomed their hair conventionally, but the pop culture that was about to explode changed all that. Young males started to interest themselves in fashion almost as much as their girlfriends did. Later that year four young Scousers, once known as the Quarrymen, would sing 'Love me do', giving birth to the Beatlemania that revolutionised the music industry. The collarless jackets and the looser hairstyles were copied by youths who also looked at the wilder, less formal attire and long, flowing locks of the Rolling Stones. An advert for Capstan cigarettes shone above the heads of the young men at a time when there were no restrictions on tobacco advertising. One slogan went, 'You are never alone with a Strand', but the industry was because cigarette ads were banned on TV in February 1965.

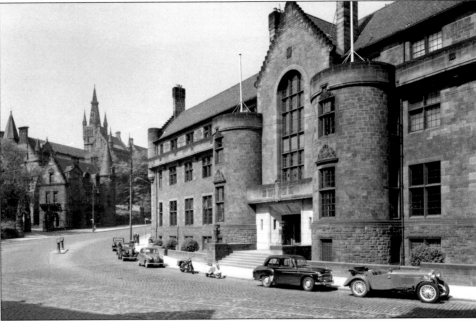

Left: Petrol rationing was still biting hard in 1948, but you would hardly have thought so for Buchanan Street was awash with cars and vans. Traffic congestion is not a modern invention, for it was with us over half a century ago. Just think how crowded this street would have been if fuel had been plentiful. Buchanan Street is just as busy today as pedestrians make their way up the hill from Argyle Street towards the Buchanan Galleries. Now closed to traffic, the street has retained the splendour of earlier times, remaining Glasgow's most important shopping area. Much of the glorious architecture that we have loved for over a century is still here for us to enjoy. Frasers is a massive department store formed from the combination of a number of old warehouses, the Prince of Wales Buildings (Princes Square) have stood since 1854 and Argyll Arcade retains its French style appeal with jewellers' shops under its iron, timber and glass frame. The huge throngs out on Buchanan Street over 50 years ago had the same motives as those to be found there today. True, some came to shop, but many others were there to soak up the atmosphere on Glasgow's most vibrant of streets. The removal of choking exhaust fumes when it was pedestrianised has made just being here the most enjoyable of experiences.

Top: A university education was available to people from all walks of life, even in 1956.

The transport parked outside the students' union building suggested that toffs wearing cravats had rolled up in their open topped tourers to rub shoulders with lesser mortals in baby Austins or on two wheelers. The motorbike and scooter parked side by side on the corner of University Avenue and Kelvin Way suggested that two friends had arrived at the same time to enjoy a drink at the bar or indulge in more heavy yard of ale contests. A decade later these vehicles would be the symbols of bitter rivalry as greasy haired rockers on high powered motorcycles roared off to pitched battles with mods on Lambrettas and Vespas. During the mid to late 60s every Bank Holiday was punctuated with reports of bicycle chain wielding thugs fighting it out with equally stupid youths who were not averse to using knives. There was none of that in the university union, for disagreement was conducted via reasoned debate, or so the students informed us. The Beer Bar in the basement, if the truth were to be known, had been more than a little lively in the days before the soothing influence of female students was allowed. This formation of a mixed union did not take place until the early 1980s, so there was nearly a century of male waywardness for them to correct! The men's union was formed in 1885, though this building is much more recent, having been completed in 1931. Students originally used the McIntyre Building, further along University Avenue, that later was given over to the women's union.

Below: A salt market was established here in medieval times mainly for the use of fishermen on the Clyde who needed a preservative for their catch. The street retains the name that connects it to those days, though Saltmarket becomes High Street as it approaches the Tolbooth Steeple at Glasgow Cross. At one time the road swung away to the right as it reached Bridgegate and on this corner the first tenements built as part of the Glasgow Improvement Trust were erected in 1880. The homes did not have their own toilets, residents having to share two on each landing. By 1958 there had been a great deal of improvement in the living conditions Glaswegians enjoyed as the notorious slums were being replaced by new housing estates and some of the old tenement buildings were remodelled into more comfortable and better class accommodation. It was a period when Scotland and the rest of Britain began to feel as if the austere postwar years really were a thing of the past. We had money in our pockets, unemployment had fallen and bright, new consumer goods, such as washing machines and televisions appeared in an increasing number of ordinary homes, making life easier and more entertaining. The main problem on Saltmarket related to the heavy traffic grinding to a halt, but this was common across the city.

Right: Sauchiehall Street gets part of its name from the sallows or willow trees that once grew in this area. Their name in local dialect would have been 'saughs'. The second portion has nothing to do with any grand hall or mansion that might have been in the vicinity, but relates to the haughs or meadows over which the path was originally trodden. Mispronunciation or an attempt by people with origins south of the border to anglicise the word meant that 'haugh' was wrongly changed to 'hall'. Looking east from the crossroads with Campbell Street and Cambridge Street towards the far end of Sauchiehall Street, the part beyond West Nile Street was once known as Cathcart Street. The trams and cars that travelled along the roadway in 1950 have long gone as all traffic has been removed from this now pedestrianised part of Glasgow. The Savoy Shopping Centre has since appeared on the left, though it has retained the frontage that was once the Cumming and Smith Building, with its grand columns rising up through three storeys to the beautifully designed figures above, crafted by WB Rhind. Sauchiehall Street is second only to Buchanan Street in its importance as a shopping area, but it was formerly a fashionable place to live when early 19th century merchants made their homes here.

Far left: You could almost be in old Athens or ancient Rome when looking at the magnificence of the architecture that produced the Royal Exchange, though the road setts, street lamps and overhead wires might spoil the illusion. Despite that, it can be appreciated as an outstanding example of Georgian work that was built in 1780 for William Cunninghame, an immensely rich tobacco merchant who paid the then mammoth sum of £10,000 for its construction. The Royal Bank of Scotland bought the mansion in 1817 and Royal Exchange Square developed around this building from 1827, when it became the centre for trading tobacco, rum and sugar. As the industrial revolution took hold, iron, coal and shipping became incorporated into its dealings. The Royal Exchange flourished for over a century before the council used it to accommodate Stirling's Library in 1949. In 1996 it was transformed into the Gallery of Modern Art and the floor where traders used to barter is now called the Earth Gallery, displaying the work of some postwar Scottish artists, for example Howson, Currie and Campbell. The mounted figure outside the old Exchange is a representation of the victor at Waterloo, Arthur Wellesley, Duke of Wellington. It was erected in 1844 and is one of many examples of the Victorians' fascination with military might as they put up countless statues and named hosts of streets after Nelson, Wellington, Garnet, Gordon and other commanders.

Left: There are peaceful, green parts to every city, though it is sometimes hard to appreciate they exist when battling with crowds of commuters in the busy centre. In 1936 this view of Glasgow University, with the Kelvingrove Art Gallery and Museum to the left, was taken from Park Terrace, where grand houses have curved away majestically since 1855. The university is one of Britain's oldest, having been established in 1451 in the cathedral by Bishop William Turnbull, with the blessing of an edict from Pope Nicholas V. The seat of learning soon moved to High Street, where it continued until the poor condition of the buildings forced relocation to Gilmorehill in 1864. The resplendent tower was the brainchild of that remarkable and prolific Victorian architect, Sir George Gilbert Scott. He restored such famous monuments as Ely, Salisbury and Lichfield cathedrals, as well as Westminster Abbey. Scott was responsible for influencing the design or restoration of almost 500 churches, 39 cathedrals and minsters and many buildings for colleges and universities. The art gallery and museum building was the centrepiece of the 1901 Exhibition that marked the 50th anniversary of the Great Exhibition at the Crystal Palace, London. Its fairytale towers, spires and turrets lend an air of make believe to its architecture that has attracted local inhabitants to it for over a century.

Top: It was only in 1938 that the Penilee district, to the west of the city, was brought within Glasgow's administrative boundaries. The three storey flats on view in Craigmuir Road in 1942 were part of the Corporation's housing stock that look quite bleak to us, but were an early attempt to provide better living accommodation for those who had grown up in overcrowded tenements and slums. Unfortunately, some of the high rise developments that went up then and later produced their own form of problems as they were impersonal and often were the breeding ground for unsavoury elements in society. That criticism could hardly be levelled at this group by the phone box, for they waited their turn patiently, discussing the best way to eke out their rations or cook that revolting pie of turnips, swedes and parsnips recommended by the Food Minister, Lord Woolton. You could bet that his lordship would be tucking into something more substantial than that in his mansion down south. The average working class family lived on a budget of £5 per week, spending about £1 15s (£1.75) of that on food. The government issued 'A kitchen goes to war', a ration-time cookery book with recipes contributed by 150 famous people, none of whom had ever tried to live on what these women had to juggle. Did any of the contributors really taste 'Blitz Broth' for themselves?

Right: People look just like little ants, scurrying hither and thither, in this elevated 1937 shot of George Square looking across at the City Chambers. It is, perhaps, Glasgow's most impressive building, which is only fitting as it is the centre of local government and is its own monument to the power and wealth of the late Victorian era. Just as sumptuous inside as well as out, it was designed by William Young and has attracted visitors from all over the world since 1890. Two noble lions guard the white Cenotaph, unveiled in 1924 as a memorial to those who fell in the Great War. The single word 'pax' (peace), by the sculpted wreath and palm frond, makes the message simple and to the point. A multitude of monuments, statues and memorials to the great and the good abound in the square. The central column is topped by a statue to one of Scotland's foremost authors, Sir Walter Scott, creator of 'Rob Roy', 'Waverley' and 'Heart of Midlothian', amongst other notable works of the early 19th century. Scott was born in Edinburgh, but many of Glasgow's famous sons are remembered elsewhere around George Square. There are statues to Thomas Campbell, Lord Clyde, Thomas Graham and Sir John Moore, as well as those to 'foreign' politicians, royals and other important figures. In 1937, office workers in the City Chambers were taking a lunch break, enjoying the sunshine on the benches with their backs to the traffic, gazing across to the 1878 Post Office and the 1870 palatial building that now houses the tourist information centre.

Events & occasions

How we showed the flag and went mad on 2 June 1953 as our monarch walked regally down the aisle of Westminster Abbey to take the Coronation Oath. Flanked by all the panoply of church and state and holding the ceremonial mace and sceptre, Queen Elizabeth II was enthroned as head of Britain and the Commonwealth. Her clear, light voice promised service to her people, a vow she has kept nobly through even the most trying of times, including her 'annus horribilis' when fire hit Windsor and Prince Charles' marriage failed. The whole ceremony was relayed to homes across the nation via BBC TV, with an accompanying commentary from Richard Dimbleby, a broadcaster who had the perfect, profound voice to match the occasion. Those lucky enough to own a television set suddenly found friends they never knew existed, as their front rooms filled with people anxious to view the scene in a flickering black and white. Large street parties were held and processional floats, like this one at Baillieston, passed by on their way to organised celebration in town and city parks. Children love dressing up and this happy gang of kiddies had great fun putting on party clothes or fancy dress and waving at their mums and dads on the streets watching them go by. 'Vivat Regina!' they cried, or the Glaswegian equivalent.

The Times pavilion was just one of the many attractions that brought people to the Empire Exhibition on more than one occasion. There was just so much to take in that a single visit could not do it all justice. The exhibition was a temporary affair and most of the delightful pavilions and edifices disappeared when it closed. The Palace of Art is the only building to remain within the park, though being turned into the sports hall has extensively altered it. The Palace of Engineering was re-erected at Prestwick Airport, but the granite block that is the Exhibition Memorial can still be seen on Bellahouston Hill and the Peace Cairn, put up as a sign of both fear and hope, is situated in front of Charles Rennie Mackintosh's House for an Art Lover. The Empire Exhibition had a number of noble objectives. It was intended to show to the world the progress made by the British Empire and the skills and potential of its members, whilst encouraging trade and friendship between them. It also hoped to stimulate Scotland by promoting its industries, tourism and history. A final wish was for the world to recognise the Empire's peaceful aspirations, but Herr Hitler did not seem to be listening. It was just as well that our armed forces had their own pavilion, though it was a sad reflection on the times that it was more popular than the Peace Pavilion.

Bellahouston Park took over from Kelvingrove the role of playing host to the city's great exhibitions as its greater acreage afforded the opportunity to put on a show grander than those that had gone before. This general view of the 1938 Empire Exhibition can only give a fraction of the idea of its extent and the amount of razzmatazz it generated. It really ought to have been called the Commonwealth Exhibition as the British Commonwealth of Nations had been born in 1931, better reflecting the self governing nations that still swore allegiance. But, in 1938, we were not as sensitive or as politically correct, so Empire Exhibition it was. Bellahouston Park was created on land that had been bought for the city around Bellahouston Hill in 1896. Glasgow had hosted exhibitions before and this one was timed to mark the 50th anniversary of the city's first, held, some said, to show those great rivals, Edinburgh and Manchester, a thing or two. The timing of this event was criticised by a few who cast an anxious eye across Europe where the spectre of war loomed ever closer, but the exhibition met the approval of the vast majority. It offered a hope for the future, set as it was against a backdrop of inner city poverty and squalor.

Above: The official opening of the Empire Exhibition was not held in Bellahouston Park, but away at Ibrox football stadium. Having carried out their official duties on 3 May 1938, King George VI and Queen Elizabeth hurried across to join these crowds on the exhibition concourse. Over 150,000 attended on the first day and many of them came back for more over the next six months. Queen Elizabeth bought two Shirley Temple dolls to take home for her daughters, Elizabeth and Margaret. It would not be a shock to learn that our current monarch still has her souvenir, for she enjoys playthings like the amusing musical fish she owns. This was the fourth large exhibition that Glasgow had mounted, following on those in 1888, 1901 and 1911. The first had been styled on the 1851 Great Exhibition at the Crystal Palace and the second, opened by Princess Louise, Duchess of Fife, gave notice of social change to come as the Women's Committee, led by Tessa Mackenzie, contributed actively towards the exhibition's success. The event in 1911 concentrated more on history and literature than the Victorian obsession with the industrial revolution, but the Empire Exhibition of 1938 was twice the size of anything that had gone before. Despite atrocious weather during the summer, over 12,000,000 visitors passed through the gates. In October, a certain Mrs Wilson received special recognition that she was the 12 millionth visitor by being presented with £10 and a gold watch. She also won a free season ticket to the exhibition, but since it closed two days after she received her award Mrs Wilson was reported as being not best pleased!

At leisure

Passengers and crew disembarking from the Queen Mary at her berth on the Clyde in 1940 were leaving one of the great monuments to the industry that had supplied the lifeblood of Glasgow and Clydeside for generations. The great liner, the first ship of over 75,000 tons, was launched in September 1934 at Clydebank, amid much popping of champagne corks. It was only right and proper that Queen Mary, the wife of George V, swung the ceremonial bottle as the liner slid down the slipway and into the water. There were two unfortunate incidents before embarking on her maiden voyage as the ship ran aground twice, but all was well on 27 May 1936 when the super liner left Southampton for Cherbourg and then on across the Atlantic to New York. The journey took over four days at a record speed of 31 knots under the watchful eye of her commander, Edgar Britten. The 1,840 privileged passengers paid a minimum of £37 5s (£37.25) for the trip of a lifetime. In August the Queen Mary claimed the Blue Riband for Britain, making the crossing in three minutes under four days, beating the record of the Normandie by over three hours. She took another four hours off the record in August 1938 and was to carry on cruising for nearly 30 years more. The Queen Mary discharged her last passenger at Southampton in September 1967, before being sailed across the ocean to start a new life at Long Beach, California.

High days and holidays, or maybe just a day trip out for the staff of the South Scotland Electricity Board in 1958. A trip down the Clyde and along the coast to Largs made for a great occasion and something of an adventure, a pleasant relief from the daily grind. We still took great pleasure in exploring our own country in the 50s, for the package holiday to Spain was still in its infancy. Many people took their annual holiday in the same place and even at the same guest house year after year. Foreign shores were thought to be those at Scarborough or Blackpool and a trip across the water meant enjoying the horse drawn trams on the front at Douglas, not the avenues and boulevards of gay 'Paree'. The staff outing was another traditional break that most of us enjoyed, for it was a chance to spend the day when management was our equal. The foreman on the shop floor or the head clerk in his office had no special standing on the deck of the steamer as it chugged down the river, for our money was just as good as theirs. Cheeky young typists often took a liberty with the boss, flashing their eyes at him and giggling with one another, but they would probably have run a mile if he had taken them up on any of their saucy suggestions. The older matrons in the party regarded themselves as being rather above that sort of behaviour, but truth to tell, they had gone through the same routines a generation earlier.

Bottom: The Hampden roar is famous the world over for the prickly sensation it creates on the backs of the necks of footballers walking from the tunnel onto the field of play. It is particularly nerve wracking for visiting teams as the combined voices in a six figure crowd rose to a crescendo of noise, loud enough to make the bravest of souls tremble. Ground capacity, because of safety measure, has been reduced, but the atmosphere remains the same. In 1955 Celtic played Clyde in the FA Cup Final at Hampden Park, a match that the former was expected to win for Celtic had picked up the trophy, beating Aberdeen the year before, and were in no mood to surrender it. In front of 106,111 supporters the teams battled out a 1-1 draw, but few neutrals thought that Clyde would match mighty Celtic in the replay. They were right, but not in the way they expected, for on the following Wednesday Clyde did not equal its rivals, but outdid them, winning 1-0. Just to prove it was no fluke, the club won in the final again in 1958 with a single goal victory over Hibs. The 1950s were quite productive for Clyde as it scored a massive 122 goals in the 1956-57 season in Division Two and Billy McPhail knocked in 32 goals in the 1951-52 season in the same division. It took Celtic a long time to recover from the shock of losing, failing to win the FA Cup once more until 1965. By then it had put together a side that was the basis of triumph in the 1967 European Cup.

Below: The Odeon at Shettleston was showing 'The End of the Affair' in 1955, a film based on the Graham Greene novel of the same name. Its stars numbered some of the finest actors of postwar cinema, Deborah Kerr, Van Johnson, John Mills and Peter Cushing. The story of a repressed wife in wartime London and her affair with a writer that brought on her religious guilt and ultimately her death was hardly the subject that would have attracted children to queue in droves. Their interests did not lie in

such turgid and sordid tales, for this was Saturday, the afternoon of the special children's matinee. For just a few pence you could escape for hours into the darkness of the stalls and enjoy a Tom and Jerry cartoon that always seemed to include the cat's outline on the wire fence through which he had been catapulted. There were comic shorts starring the Three Stooges and cowboy films with Roy Rogers singing 'Tumbling Tumbleweed' as he rode Trigger off into the sunset. Best of all were the multi part serials with Flash Gordon's space ship trailing sparks behind it as he flew across the weird terrain of some planet from outer space. Every episode ended with him in some impossible tangle or danger from which he could not possibly escape, but next week provided the miraculous release as he set off to save the world again. When the film broke down, as it often did, children drummed their feet on the floor in annoyance until the usherette played her torch beam across them, issuing dire threats of expulsion.

Top: Story time at 100 Norfolk Street was under way in 1933 at the home of the Gorbals Public Library. Eager children, their eyes sparkling with the magic of the

mystery being told to them, hung on every word. There were stories of daring deeds in the French Foreign Legion, told in PC Wren's 'Beau Geste', or the adventures of Richard Hannay as he sought to unravel the tangle of the 'Thirty-nine Steps' that John Buchan thrilled readers with. For little ones there were fairy stories, like the 'Tinderbox' that had a dog with eyes as big as saucers, or a good old standby such as 'Snow White' or 'Rumpelstiltskin'. There were tales with a moral message, as in Harriet Beecher Stowe's 'Uncle Tom's Cabin' with its anti slavery theme, or Charles Kingsley's 'Water Babies' reminding readers that life for children was often grim in the mid 19th century. Every home had a collection of books and a variety of reading matter available, for it was one of the most popular means of home entertainment we had. In the days before the goggle box appeared in the corner of every sitting room, and nowadays bedroom, and generations before computer and video games took over, we listened to the radio, played games and read books avidly. When was the last time you saw a youngster reading just for the sheer joy of losing himself inside the story?

Top: These little imps, hamming it up for the camera, were the reason that we went to war in 1939, just so that they could be free. When hostilities ended and the armed forces were demobbed families were reunited, some for the first time in six years. Not every homecoming was joyous, for in some cases new liaisons had been formed, whilst in others women had grown to enjoy their independence from male domination. So many men could not adapt to the new order and, for one reason or another, the divorce rate skyrocketed. In 1946 80,000 marriages went through the courts, leading one MP, Mr Skeffington-Lodge, to bluster that a marriage licence was worth as much as a dog licence, in terms of moral value. But, there were countless loving reunions that did not make the headlines as couples closed the door behind them and did what came naturally. It came as no surprise that the late 40s saw a baby boom as the stork put in for time and a half to be calculated in its wage packet. The trio under the tram stop on Main Street, Baillieston was born into a Britain that embraced the welfare state and grew up surrounded by free orange juice, school milk and NHS spectacles. As they said 'Cheese' for the cameraman, their parents hoped that they would be able to build a better world than the one they had forged in the first half of the 20th century.

Above: The Corporation flats at Hutchesontown were among the first housing developments undertaken by the city in the 1950s. Seen in May 1958, they included play areas where children could let off steam and exercise their boundless energies away from the dangers presented by road users. They had climbing frames, seesaws and kicking walls, with alleys for marbles and toy cars. Those overlooking the playground sometimes complained about

the noise, particularly those on nights trying to get some shuteye after a long shift, but it was better to have the children where you knew where they were. In the evening the playground sometimes attracted groups of youths, bent on mischief, but in the daylight they were places filled with happy laughter. Hutchesontown is on Rutherglen Road, to the south of the city, and takes its name from George and Thomas Hutcheson, two brothers who, in the early 17th

century, had enough love for their fellow man to provide a hospital for the aged and a system of pension payments for those in need. St David's Graveyard on Ingram Street is situated in the former orchard of the hospital and the Hutcheson name also lives on in the nearby Hutchesons' Hall. It was built for the brothers as offices and a meeting place and their statues, brought from their original site at the hospital, are situated at the front.

History lessons

Our schooldays. The happiest days of our lives according to the often repeated saying. And they probably were, though many of us took leave to doubt it at the time. How often did we hear those less than comforting words issuing forth from the mouth of some wrinkle-browed adult when we sweated complainingly over our algebra homework or struggled with irregular French verbs? How could they possibly be the best days of our lives? What did adults know about life? Rather a lot as it turned out.

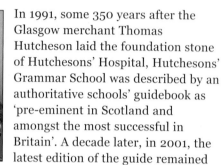

As we grow older and meet life's challenges, as we struggle in our meetings with triumph and disaster, we do eventually begin to realise that our schooldays were indeed halcyon days. And we happily pass on the wisdom of our forefathers to the next generation, telling our own sometimes incredulous offspring that these, the fleeting days of their youth, are indeed the best of their lives.

But as in all things in life for some their schooldays were better than for others. Some, on looking back, will inevitably have reason to recall their old school more fondly than others. And one school which seems to have more than its fair share of happy memories for ex-pupils is Glasgow's Hutchesons' Grammar School - Hutchie to those most familiar with this long-established institution.

In 1991, some 350 years after the Glasgow merchant Thomas Hutcheson laid the foundation stone of Hutchesons' Hospital, Hutchesons' Grammar School was described by an authoritative schools' guidebook as 'pre-eminent in Scotland and amongst the most successful in Britain'. A decade later, in 2001, the latest edition of the guide remained eulogistic: 'This is old fashioned teaching, with enormous breadth, at its very best. It's awesome, fiercely academic,

Above: Sculptures of Thomas Hutcheson (left) and George Hutcheson. Below: The Crown Street site, 1904.

but children achieve their impressive grades from a fairly unselective background'. A school that begun in the mid 17th century in a 30 square yard basement in the wing of a home for 'aigit and decreppit' men had become the second largest independent school, and one of the most impressive educational institutions, in the whole United Kingdom.

At the start of the new millennium, the school, with its multi-million pound science block, state of the art computing, technology and graphic design facilities, its much coveted sports hall and splendid new library, could hardly appear more different from the first Hutchesons' School. But the capacity of the institution to transform itself to meet the challenges presented by changing social circumstances has always been a principal factor in its success. Indeed there has not been one single Hutchesons' School: there have been several, each firmly imbued with the meritocratic Scottish tradition, and standing proudly in the vanguard of Scottish educational progress.

George Hutcheson, a successful lawyer and private banker, and his younger brother Thomas, a teacher who later turned to law, were members of a prominent Glasgow family which had acquired extensive tracts of land around the city. George Hutcheson's charitable foundation for the care of the elderly, Hutchesons' Hospital in the Trongate, was supplemented in 1641 by Thomas who made provision for extra funding to lodge and educate 'tuelf maill children indigent orphanes or uthers of lyk conditions'. Surprisingly the stipulated twelve male children, indigent orphans and others of like condition took some time to round up. Though perhaps it is not so surprising when one recalls that this was a turbulent period for both Scotland, and indeed the whole of the British Isles, after Charles I persecuted puritans and provoked revolt by the Scots. Such high handedness would only be brought to a conclusion by civil war and Charles' execution in 1649.

The first pupil was enrolled in 1643 but it was not until 1650 that the full complement of 12 had been achieved. The boys, aged from 7 to 11 years were boarded at the back

Top: *Scottish Schools Soccer Shield winners 1908.*
Left: *Hutchesons' Hall Ingram Street.*

wing of the Hospital. The school soon fell into financial difficulties, though, largely created by overspending by the Hospital Patrons in 1650 when they bought the land of the Gorbals. The school was forced to close in 1652; miraculously the building survived the Great fire of Glasgow in June of that year, an inferno which raged down the High Street for four days.

The school was re-opened in 1661 and six years later the roll had again reached its one dozen pupils. A radical and permanent change, though, was that the pupils were no longer boarders, receiving in lieu maintenance money and clothes. There may have been no cinema or television to distract pupils from their studies in those far off days but there was certainly plenty of background colour for those early 'Hutchie' boys. Bull-baiting was freely indulged in by the populace in the inner yard of the Trongate Hospital, and the Patrons also let out the main hall to dancing and fencing masters for their public lessons.

When the Hospital building in the Trongate was sold in 1795 the pupils were temporarily housed in rented premises. With the building of the imposing structure which stands resplendent in Ingram Street to this day, accommodation again became available - albeit that only a rather mean room erected at the east end of the building, and not its Grand Hall, was designated the schoolroom.

Over the course of decades the demand for education had begun to increase. Scotland would be in the vanguard of the nations which made up the British Isles when it came to providing a sound education. Not surprising then that demand for places at Hutchie had begun to exceed the twelve original places, with many parents being willing to pay for the privilege of having their sons included in the school's roll. Eventually the number of such fee paying pupils would far exceed the twelve provided for by Thomas Hutcheson.

By 1815, the year of Waterloo, the roll had risen to 76. By 1839 it stood at 120 which prompted the Patrons' decision to build a new school in Crown Street, Gorbals. The location was described as 'possessing quietness of situation, good air and a roomy open site'. The new building was opened in 1841.

Boys entering the school at the age of seven or eight received four years' elementary schooling, comprising the three R's (with a little Latin thrown in for the cleverer boys) in classes sometimes containing as many as 80 pupils. They were later apprenticed to a trade as specified in Thomas Hutcheson's will 'to be chapmen or mariners or any other lawful trade'. The boys employed had their apprentice fees paid and were given one year's maintenance money and a new suit of clothes 'for their better help and advancement to an honest life'.

Above: Drill Sergeant John Muirhead.
Left: Kingarth Street, class 4B, 1928.

Pupils showing academic promise in advance of the average were sent to the Grammar School (later the Boys High School) at the Patrons' expense to complete their education for four years to university entrance standard.

A radical change came over the school's educational outlook in 1872 with the Act of Parliament setting up compulsory education in Scotland. Entrance was no longer limited to 'foundationers': the Patrons were empowered to charge moderate fees and schooling was now provided to university entrance standard. Enshrined within the statute was the principle of enabling the finest education to be attainable for those of limited financial means. The fees were to be 'so adjusted as to place the education offered not merely within the reach of the well-to-do persons but of all classes who may be wishful to secure for their sons the advantage of the highest culture and glad to sacrifice a little in its attainment'. The school was to become a secondary school, the 'High School of the South Side' as the preceptor of the time put it, and would be open to both boys and girls.

The accommodation at Crown Street was considerably enlarged and more staff engaged. But the idea of bringing girls into the Boys' School was abandoned after heated debate and a separate Girls' School was established in a building in Elgin Street, formerly used by the Gorbals Youth School. Both schools rapidly established a high academic reputation. As early as 1880, the first year when pupils could go forward direct to the Glasgow University Bursary Competition, 'Hutchie' boys took the first three places along with another four in the first thirteen. There were very few years thereafter, for over a century, that pupils from both schools gained fewer than 20 places in the first hundred. In one astonishing annus mirabilis, 1955, seven places in the first twelve went to Hutchesonians, boys taking 1st, 2nd, 4th and 7th places with the girls taking 3rd, 9th and 11th places.

Above: *P1 and P2, 1936.*
Below: *Kingarth Street infants class, 1938-1939.*

The story of the Hutchesons' schools since 1872 has not, however, been without its moments of crisis. At the outset the numbers soared to over 1,000 boys and 800 girls, but a number of factors precipitated a sharp decline: increasing educational competition, the increasingly depressing ambience of the Gorbals and the lack of facilities in the cramped girls' quarters in the Elgin Street building. By 1902 the number of fee-paying pupils had sunk to just 161 boys and 213 girls. Stung into action the Patrons decided to invest in the future and secured land at Kingarth Street and Crosshill: the grand building which today houses the combined junior school was opened as the girls' school by Lord Balfour of Burleigh on 31 January 1912.

The new girls' school was successful from the start amply fulfilling its purpose of providing for the 'Higher Education of girls' whilst simultaneously training them 'in all womanly accomplishments'. Many distinguished women owed much to their Kingarth Street start in life: Anna Buchan - the novelist O Douglas and the sister of John Buchan; Madge E Anderson the first woman in the UK to become a solicitor, the artist Edith Craig, and in the world of music Dorothy Parsons, Florence McBride and Mabel Ritchie whilst others such as Jean Taylor Smith, Kathleen Garscadden and Eileen McCallum would find fame on the radio and the stage.

The Boys' Grammar School too began its slow climb back to its position of former glory. It was fortunate in its Rectors: Thomas Menzies (1861-1902), Dr W King Gillies, Dr JC Scott, W Tod Ritchie scholar, sportsman and man of affairs, James A Watson and John M Hutchison. There were only six changes of Rectorship in 100 years. They

Top: *School Council 1954.*
Above: *A senior Hutchie girls' class in the late 1930s.*

were assisted by many distinguished dominies: Sergeant John Muirhead, Drill Sergeant for 38 years, Alexander Bonar 41 years, Andrew Pringle 35 years, and above all James Caddell possibly the greatest teacher and certainly the greatest character who ever taught in Hutchie, 38 years.

There would be many famous former pupils: John Buchan, Lord Tweedmuir, novelist and MP, Lord High Commissioner, Lord Chancellor of Edinburgh University, Governor General of Canada and a man who in his remarkable variety of achievement can almost be taken to sum up in one person the astonishing diversity that has characterised the product of Hutchesons'. Two Lord Provosts of Glasgow, Sir Alexander B Swan and Sir Myer Galpern were Hutchie boys whilst the spirit of the school penetrated the House of Commons in the emphatic character of James Maxton.

Business has been well represented by Lord McGowan of ICI. In sport Willie Edward captained Scotland at cricket for many years, Graham Everett and Alan Paterson were household names in athletics. The church was also prominently represented by Principal Mauchline of Trinity College Glasgow the Very Reverend Professor Daniel Lamont, ex Moderator of the Church of Scotland, and by the Reverend JM MacLennan an ex Moderator of the Free Church of Scotland.

To grow and improve its facilities, however, buildings as well as pupils were important. As early as 1914 it had become clear that the only way forward for the Boys' School was a new building. The beginning of the Great War in that year, however, did not make it the most auspicious time to contemplate new construction projects. Even after the end of the first world war, in 1918, continuing financial problems and lack of entrants rendered that move impossible for some time. It was not to be until 1938, yet another equally inauspicious year, that the Scottish Education Department approved the purchase of a site at Crossmyloof. The outbreak of the second world war in 1939 however gave Crown Street another quarter century of life and Crossmyloof was turned over to allotments. Work would not resume on the new building until 1956.

The new buildings, the fourth home of the Boys' School, were formally inaugurated by Sir Thomas

Below: *A 1950s Kingarth Street Science Lab.*

Innes, Lord Lyon King of Arms, on 11th May 1960. A Founders' Day, to be subsequently celebrated annually in Glasgow Cathedral, was begun in 1961 by Rector John Hutchison with the stated aim of forming an image of the past in the minds of the present. 'I hope that this day will serve to perpetuate the old traditions and to stimulate school loyalties' the Rector said to the assembled pupils, staff, trustees and guests. Hutchison was constantly concerned to protect the school's traditions, not least the original 'Mortification' - that none were to be excluded through lack of means. The Rector, however, was not the only person interested in ensuring that a good education was available to everyone regardless of their circumstances.

The 1960s brought political threats to many historic schools as Labour pursued a comprehensive-only policy. In 1967 the Labour Secretary of State froze grants to all 29 Scottish grant-aided schools including Hutchie. One way forward was an amalgamated co-educational school and this was eventually achieved in 1976, with the combined schools becoming fully independent in 1985.

Rector David Ward presided over the 350th Anniversary celebrations in 1991. The event was launched with overwhelming support, so much so that the Rector was able to report 'All the correspondence we have had, the enthusiasms that have been shown and the flood of reminiscences it has released indicate the affection and respect that former pupils have had for their school. It mattered to them.'

The Rt. Hon Lord McColl of Dulwich, Professor of Surgery, University of London delivered the Founders' Day address in that 350th Anniversary year and highlighted the key features of the Hutchesonian tradition: an ethos of high expectation from both staff and pupils, a demand for high standards, for excellence without arrogance from everyone associated with the institution, a

performance ethic of sensible stretching as the expected norm for everyone in their academic and extra-curricular endeavours. 'Mediocrity is something which Hutchesonians have never been allowed to accept. Don't settle for anything less than your full, God-given potential. God has made you a unique person, by your genetic endowment, upbringing and education. He means you to be fulfilled, not frustrated. His purpose is that everything you are should be stretched in His service, and in the service of others'. Marvellous words in an age when so often young people are not asked to do enough; when it is too readily forgotten that youngsters actively enjoy being pushed to the limits of their potential.

Above left: *Kingarth Street infants, 1980s.*
Below: *Founders' Day Address at Glasgow Cathedral, 19th March 1991.*

The 1990s was a decade of building development for the Hutchesons' sites. The start of the new millennium saw a further transformation: Hutchesons' was approached by the Governors of Laurel Park School concerned about the viability of their famous establishment; a merger took place in August 2001 with the Laurel Park site immediately converted into the new co-educational Hutchesons' Lilybank Junior School. The new Laurel Park Sports Centre in Anniesland, comprising sports hall, Astroturf pitch and squash courts, partly funded by the National Lottery, also came under the Hutchesons' umbrella.

'Who knows how future generations will view the achievements and aspirations of the school in the early years of the 21st century?' asks Rector John Knowles. 'Whatever, they cannot but be impressed by the seemingly endless enthusiasm, energy and successes of the pupils and staff.'

Hutchesons' continues to produce eminent men and women. In recent times celebrated former pupils have included Lord Irvine of Lairg, the Lord Chancellor, TV personality Carol Smillie, rugby internationals Gordon and Alan Bulloch, and mobile phone millionaire Richard Emanuel of DX Communications.

Perhaps sometimes they recall the last verse of the Old Boys' school song penned by Robert Bain: 'So when you pass by the old school where/The brothers stand in stone/If you hear the beat of invisible feet/ and the sound of trumpet blown/Salute! 'Tis the tread of the long since dead. Cap off! It's the march of the clan/ Who lived and wrought in the pride of the thought/ They were Hutchesonian'. The torch of learning, still shining brightly after more than three centuries, continues to be passed down to each new generation of pupils - the Hutchie legend lives on, inexorably leading each old boy and girl to the ultimate discovery that our schooldays are indeed the best days of our lives.

Top: *The school's Crossmyloof site, pictured in 1980.*
Above: *The new Science Block, 1991.*

Bird's eye view

Port Dundas is situated at the end of the final section of the Forth and Clyde Canal that connected Scotland's east and west coasts for cross country navigation in 1790. It was used commercially until 1963, though enthusiasts and pleasure craft still use some of its waters and basins with hopes that one day the whole canal can be navigated again. Port Dundas was Glasgow's most prestigious port until Rennie and Telford deepened the Clyde at the beginning of the 19th century. It took its name from Lawrence Dundas, the governor of the canal's Navigation Company. Before shipbuilding became the mainstay of the economy, Glasgow invested heavily in cotton manufacture, as suited its damp climate. Further back, into the 17th and 18th centuries, tobacco helped establish it as the 'second city of the Empire', bringing great prosperity to the merchants or 'tobacco lords'. The aerial view from Port Dundas, looking westward, is a fine example of the built up nature of the city that began to gasp for space as a seemingly never ending spate of buildings came to dominate the skyline. As the importance of shipbuilding waned, manufacturing of textiles, food and beverages, chemicals, engineering and printing became important in the economy. Nowadays, modern industrial estates house many small firms, whilst others have moved to Glasgow's new towns.

In the early 1930s, for a while shipbuilding on the Clyde remained a major source of employment for Glasgow people, though the great days of the late 19th century would never return. The depression years meant that there were periods when unemployment was high, but there were also occasions, thanks to naval contracts and special projects, when the order books filled again. Then, the warehouses were full and the giant cranes swung to and fro busying about their work, as in this scene at Govan, repeated up and down the river. Shipbuilding was not an isolated industry, for so many other trades went hand in glove with it. Joiners and carpenters, boilermakers and electricians, carpet manufacturers and engine builders all found employment connected with the yards, as well as an army of clerical and support staff. When shipbuilding fell into major decline in the second half of the century the knock on effect was felt across the board because of the huge numbers who had to rely upon the work in the yards for their livelihood. Competition from Tyneside and abroad, coupled with a failure to have a proper policy of reinvestment did not help and Glasgow also struggled to match work being carried out closer to home. The yards at Clydebank claimed a share of the industry, with the launch of its Cunard White Star liner, Queen Mary, by her namesake on 26 September 1934 being one of the most notable events of the era.

As we look from the university tower the view takes in part of the northwest of the city suburbs as they appeared in 1937. The rolling countryside in the distance acts as a marked contrast to the built up areas stretching out towards the distant hills. During the industrial revolution the population increased enormously as immigrants from the Highlands in the 1820s and from Ireland in the 1840s provided the unskilled labour required. King Cotton employed almost a third of the Glasgow's workforce, but like the tobacco industry, it was to be badly affected by external factors. The American Civil War and intense competition from cities like

Manchester and Bradford saw Glasgow turn its attention to more diverse activity, particularly in shipbuilding. During the 19th century the population exploded, increasing by 1,000 per cent to around 750,000 by the start of the Edwardian era. When the cameraman climbed this tower the figure had grown to one in excess of 1,000,000. All the time new districts were being brought under the city's control, adding both to Glasgow's influence but also to its difficulties in managing such a huge area. What had been 716 hectares from Anderston to James Street and West Nile Street to Camlachie in 1800 became over 16,000 hectares by the outbreak of World War II.

Above: This 1937 view from the university tower looks towards the city centre across Kelvin Way. Kelvingrove Park has been providing escapism from the grime of the city since the council acquired land on the eastern side of the river in 1852, originally calling it West End Park. When the university was established to the west of the River Kelvin, further land was added. Working to a design by Wilson and Kyle, trees were planted and paths laid, providing the attractive walks and scenery that have been a joy to behold ever since. With such a large expanse of parkland to enjoy, Kelvingrove Park has never seemed crowded, other than when national and international exhibitions were held. Lovers appreciated the quiet, open spaces in which to conduct their trysts, children ran merrily across the lawns and picnickers stretched out in the sunshine listening to bands playing Gilbert and Sullivan melodies, songs from the shows or rousing Souse marches. Dotted around the park are various sculptures, including one of the writer Thomas Carlyle and another of Lord Roberts, of Indian mutiny fame. The fountain to the left centre, topped with a statue of Sir Walter Scott's 'Lady of the Lake' was dedicated in 1872 to Robert Stewart, the main instigator of the plan to improve the city's water supply by bringing fresh supplies from Loch Katrine in the 1850s.

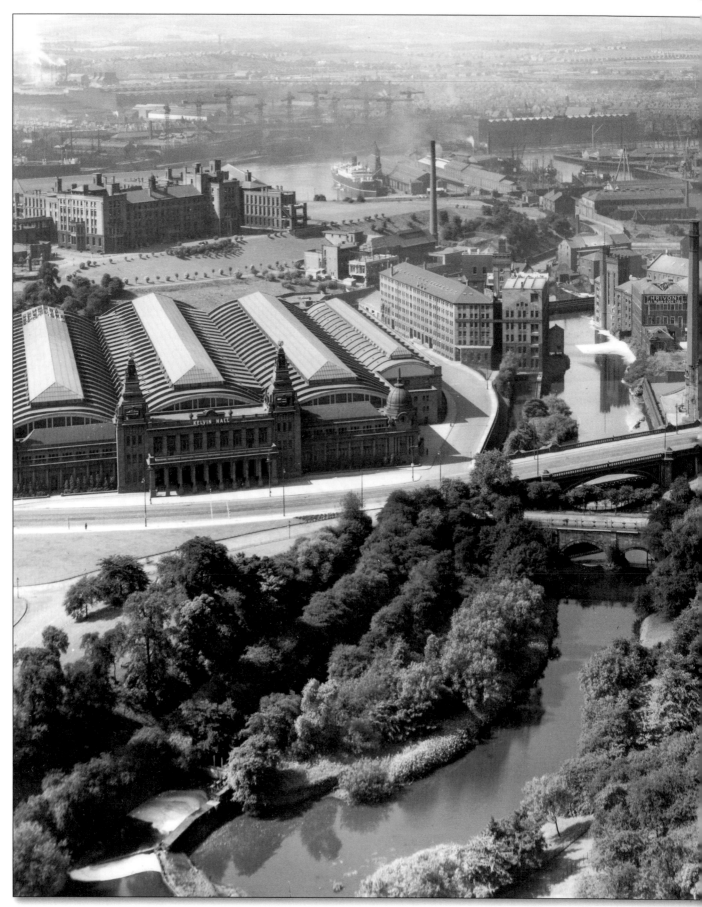

Left: As the River Kelvin heads for the elbow that takes it north towards Wyndford and Maryhill, it passes Kelvin Hall on Dumbarton Road. It was built in 1927 By TPM Somers and presents an impressive face to passers-by with its majestic towers, globes and obelisks. In 1937 it had just completed its first decade as a mighty exhibition centre that would continue to provide excellent service to the city until the mid 1980s when the Scottish Exhibition and Conference Centre (SECC) opened, to the west of the city centre close to the Clyde. Kelvin Hall had nearly 60 years of prominence, hosting numerous major exhibitions and conferences and was also the site for the annual carnival held every Christmas. During the second world war it was requisitioned for government use as a factory, with its massive floor space being used for the manufacture of barrage balloons. When the much larger SECC took over its role as an exhibition centre the rear of Kelvin Hall was converted into the Museum of Transport and the front was revamped as the International Sports Arena, providing excellent facilities for both athletes from all over the world as well as local inhabitants. Although its focus has changed, Kelvin Hall continues to provide an integral part of Glasgow activity.

Below: Wellington Church, in the foreground, on University Avenue, by Southpark Avenue, was built in the style of a late Greek revival temple by TL Watson for the United Presbyterian Church in 1884. The idea of raising the building above street level on a podium was first used by University College of London and also has some similarities of design with the Parisian Church of St Madeleine. A grand organ, built by Foster and Andrews of Hull, is housed inside, under an ornately plastered ceiling. Further north, beyond Wellington Church, the quaint shape of Hillhead High School is one of the most striking buildings that can be identified. Its open galleries were laid out in a butterfly plan, common to many schools of that era, and, when this photograph was taken in 1937, had only been established here for six years. Built in bright red brick, there were four classroom wings of two or three storeys splaying out from a central block. The open corridors seemed to draw icy winds like a magnet and students and teachers had to be both hardy and intelligent to get on in the world. Further back, along Great Western Road, were Cooper's Building, a high class grocer's, and Hubbard's shop and restaurant. Both were later turned into pubs.

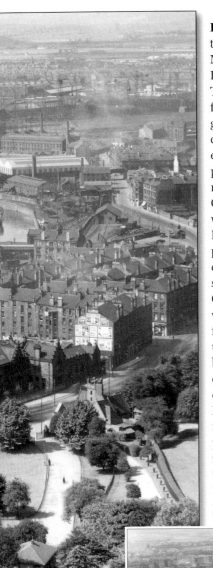

The aerial view of the 1938 Empire Exhibition in Bellahouston Park shows the imagination and style of the architects who designed the buildings that were to attract so much interest in the six months that it dominated the southwest of the city. The name of the architect in chief, Thomas Smith Tait, is still remembered by some today because the 300 foot Tower of Empire that stood on top of Bellahouston Hill was nicknamed 'Tait's Tower' in his honour. Sadly, it was taken down in 1939 as it was too obvious a landmark that would have given enemy aircraft an easy navigational reference point. Only its

foundation's remain in situ. On the day in May that King George VI and Queen Elizabeth officially opened the exhibition, Hitler and Mussolini were meeting in Rome to form a Fascist pact. The buildings or pavilions had a distinctive look about them and individual countries and commercial interests added their own stamp to them as they advertised their importance in the world. The South Africans made sure that their pavilion stood out as it was constructed in a colonial style, rather than in the modern manner of most of the others. After the exhibition, the South African pavilion was used by ICI as a staff canteen at Ardeer.

On the move

The A82, Great Western Road, runs up the hill towards Kelvinside, past the Botanic Gardens. In 1931 the nanny pushing the box-like pram in through the main gate was heading towards the two brick houses that were erected in 1904. She was off to spend some time admiring the Kibble Palace, dating from 1873 when it was brought here from John Kibble's home at Coulport. Its impressive dome originally sheltered a concert hall and auditorium in which the Victorian prime ministers Gladstone and Disraeli both addressed audiences. It was converted into a home for plants from across the planet in 1881 and is just one of the many attractions in the Botanic Gardens. This site replaced gardens near Sauchiehall Street when plants and greenhouses were transferred from there in 1839, by the Royal Botanic Institution of Glasgow, onto land purchased seven years before. The nanny and her young charge would have been able to spend many happy hours wandering through the various gardens and herbaceous borders as they meandered along the river walk by the Kelvin with its attractive Kirklee Bridge and Humpback Bridge. She shared a private moment with the baby, telling her about how she strolled along the same path on her day off, arm in arm with her sweetheart. Nanny smiled a secret smile as she remembered the daisy chain they fashioned and the promises made as the seeds were blown off dandelion clocks, saying, 'He loves me, he loves me not'.

The war was over and some semblance of normality had returned to Buchanan Street, looking north along it from Argyle Street in 1946. The sight of horse drawn vehicles rolled back the years for those who remembered when the noble steed dominated the highways at the beginning of the century, pulling wagons, trams, carts and carriages. But it was not a nostalgic longing for the old days that brought Dobbin out of retirement, it was something of a necessity as petrol and diesel supplies were scarce. Rather than give up the ghost, some traders and travellers turned back the clock and Buchanan Street echoed to the sound of clip-clopping hooves once again. As the horses moved away from the city centre gardeners living in the outskirts were glad to see them pass by for, armed with bucket and shovel, there was an instant source of fertiliser for the rhubarb readily available. Out of town it was still a common sight to see the rag and bone men with their horses and carts even in the 1950s. Just like Steptoe and Son, with their loyal servant Hercules between the shafts, they toured the streets, riding a version of side saddle on their carts as their legs dangled over the sides, calling out to housewives to bring their unwanted junk into the street. This was recycling in its crudest form, but families were happy to make an exchange of cast offs for something with which to donkeystone the front step.

Above: Even Hercules himself, never mind his bicycle, could have done anything other than wring his hands in sheer frustration at this chaotic part of Renfield Street with West George Street. For those involved in the horrific congestion there must have seemed to be little hope of progress across or out of the city for some considerable time. This was only early in the 1950s, so imagine how bad it really got as more and more cars joined the trams and buses clogging up the centre before someone said, 'Enough!' Shopping was a dirty business,

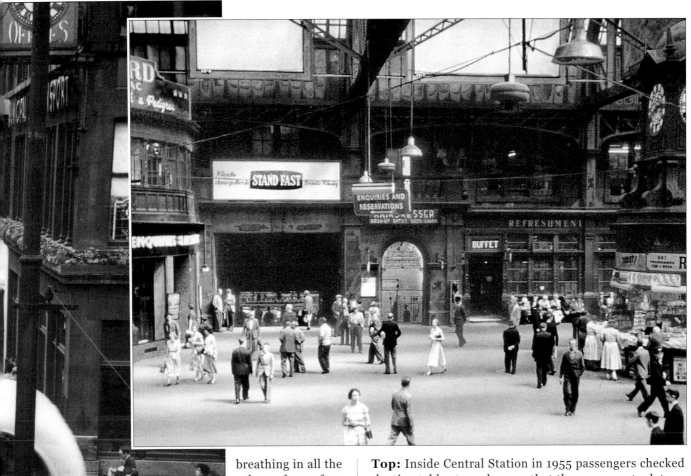

breathing in all the exhaust fumes from the cars, lorries and buses, though at least the trams ran on a clean fuel. Homes using coal fires added to the air pollution and from November through the winter there were often days when fog turned into industrial smog, clogging throats and giving those with respiratory problems a hard time. A succession of Clean Air Acts at national and local level helped clear the skies and keep collars and cuffs clean. Housewives used to despair that a freshly starched shirt or blouse only lasted a short time before becoming grimy and being thrust back into the laundry basket almost as quickly as it had left the ironing board.

Top: Inside Central Station in 1955 passengers checked the timetables to make sure that they were up to date and their train was leaving when they thought it would. It is not something we need do in the 21st century, for we can be positive that the modern service will be cancelled, arrive four hours late or set off tomorrow sometime. This is called progress. The railway was once Britain's pride and joy, but it is now a sorry tale of under achievement resulting in a total lack of public confidence. Yet, this was the revolutionary transport we pioneered in the early Victorian era. We kept ahead of the rest with magnificent locomotives and reliable rolling stock, so much so that the LNER London-Newcastle express ran at over 100 mph in 1935, in 1937 the Silver Jubilee topped 112 mph and the Coronation Scot cut the London to Edinburgh time down to six hours, with the mighty Mallard recording a remarkable 128 mph in 1938. More than 60 years on we would be lucky if a train even left the station. Central Station at Gordon Street was built for Caledonia Railway in 1839 and was extended to 13 platforms in 1906 by the company's chief engineer, Donald Mathieson. The concourse was a lively, atmospheric place, with its timber indicator board, matching ticket offices, restaurant and waiting rooms. It was built at a high level to cope with bridging the Clyde and was modernised in the 1980s.

Buchanan Street, looking north from Argyle Street, had virtually ground to a halt in 1964, so heavy were the demands made by traffic on the city's premier shopping street. It is all pedestrianised now, but the traffic in human form is just as congested as ever with people spending their money here or making their way up the hill towards the Buchanan Galleries, that modern complex of shops that covers 600,000 square feet and opened at the end of the last century. Large malls, hypermarkets and stack 'em high, sell 'em cheap stores were still to come in 1964, though supermarkets had begun to make their mark, squeezing out the traditional retailers. The swinging 60s had not yet arrived for the group of pedestrians on the left, waiting to risk life and limb in attempting to cross the road. The men had short haircuts and still went to the barber. They bought their suits at Burton's and wore homburgs or trilbies, whilst many of their wives still thought it not quite the done thing to go out bareheaded. But, as Bob Dylan put it, the times were a-changing. Four mopheads from Liverpool had already taken the musical world by storm and even staid Glaswegian males soon began to let their hair creep down towards their collars and risk the scorn of their fellows by entering the world of the unisex hairdresser. Mary Quant had her effect from far off Carnaby Street and hemlines became little more than pelmets as legs came into fashion in a big way.

This was the view from the top deck of a trolleybus heading north along Buchanan Street as it reached the junction with St Vincent Street. Note the full length of the woman's dress in the foreground as she crosses the road, setting the date as 1950. Women tired of the short hemlines forced upon them as austerity measures during the war and were glad to have the freedom to be able to wear feminine rather than utilitarian styles. In 1947 dress designer Christian Dior introduced his sensational New Look, sweeping women off their feet with its hourglass shape and use of lavish lengths of material. The ultra feminine look, with its figure of eight styling, was in and the square shoulders of the early 40s were definitely on the way out. Women worked hard undertaking male roles during the war, but it was now time for them to be cherished for their gender once more. Department stores and dress shops gradually copied the Paris fashions and brought them into the High Streets of Britain. New materials, such as rayon, corduroy and other manmade fibres added further zest to the change that swept through a woman's wardrobe. Well defined waists and mid calf soft skirts dominated the clothes pegs as the public thanked Dior for freeing them from the fuddy-duddy styles of old. France awarded him the Legion of Honour for revitalising the fashion industry.

Above: In 1950 trolleybuses on Glasgow's streets were a fairly recent innovation, as they had only been introduced to complement the tramcars and double deckers the previous year. They were a period piece that lasted less than 20 years, never being taken into city folklore as was the case with the tram service. A bizarre mix of bus and tram, with that pantograph arm reaching up greedily to suck the electricity from the overhead cables, the trolleybuses moved through the city like some quiet, avenging angels. Pedestrians feared them, because there was little sound of their approach, unlike the noise of the diesel engined buses or the clanking machinery of the tram. Accidents were often the result of a mixture of the trolleybus arriving silently and the pedestrian acting carelessly. The Corporation took great care to make sure that its transport was mechanically sound and stable. Rigorous testing of the vehicles' ability to corner well and remain upright in a crash was carried out, as here where a

trolleybus is being tilted deliberately in order to establish how well it could perform. A concentrated effort to improve public transport was made after the war when the rise in private car ownership began to congest the city streets. The rail and bus services were improved and in 1960 the suburban electrified rail network was opened, with one man-operated buses appearing a few years later. By the end of the 1990s, around 40 per cent of all journeys were made on public transport, with bus passengers outnumbering those on the railways by four to one.

Above: This AEC Regent Corporation motor bus, pictured in 1955, appears at first view to be going about its normal business. Only on closer inspection do you realise that someone is using a rather more rudimentary method than that shown in the larger picture on this page to measure how far the bus leans over with the camber of the road. The string and house brick dangling from the side of the bus demonstrates that a driver who pulled in too close to the kerb would nicely demolish the telegraph pole, or the bus, or both! And if there were any second opinions needed to the outcome of this somewhat Heath Robinson experiment, look no further than the inevitable collection of onlookers ranging from the Trilby-hatted gentlemen to the short-trousered local children.

Top: The passengers on the top deck of the tram needed the lights on full as they read their evening papers, full of the news that Marilyn Monroe had been found dead in bed at her Hollywood bungalow, an empty bottle of Nembutal sleeping tablets by her side. It was a rainy night in 1962 as the road under Central Station bridge on Argyle Street glistened, reflecting the headlights and spots of the traffic making its way past the place where people from the Highlands, recently arrived in the city seeking work, used to congregate. They sheltered from the rain on days like these and the nickname of the 'Hielanman's Umbrella' was born. Churchgoers also used it as a place to meet up with friends on their way home from morning service. There is now a collection of fast food outlets and amusement centres offering what passes for refreshment and entertainment these days. The bridge is a reconstruction of an older one carrying the old Caledonian railway and was built by McDowell, Steven & Co at the start of the last century. Perhaps the honour of being the most impressive of the railway bridges in the vicinity belongs to the Caledonia Railway Bridge, spanning the Clyde I between Glasgow Bridge and King George V Bridge. Designed by Donald Mathieson and built around the same time as the Hielanman's Umbrella, it carries 10 tracks across its complex of girders and pillars.

Below centre: We Scots like things to be neat and tidy, so perhaps this is why the quartet on the top deck of the Coronation tram sat in an ordered fashion, one behind the other. These passengers even took their seats next to the window to make everything just so. The Coronation trams, a common sight on Glasgow's streets from the late 1930s onwards, were part of a new line, having replaced the older and less reliable Standards. The last trams were large people carriers as the Coronation class of 1950 measured 35 feet by 7 feet and was 15 ft high. Weighing 16 tons, it transported 70 people. Trams, in one form or another, served the city for nearly a century, dating back to the horse drawn service that began in the 1870s. Their tracks cut straight lines down the cobbled roads, though Buchanan Street resisted their intrusion into its elegant area. The tramcars became part and parcel of Glasgow life, so much so that people just spoke of them as the 'caurs', giving them a nickname as you would an old friend. The sight of trams, two and three abreast in their heyday, dominating the city streets were as much a part of Glasgow as the gondola is to Venice. Yet, the Council, in its wisdom, called time on another piece of tradition, consigning it to a final resting place in the Transport Museum. Congested streets and traffic gridlocks, with the rise in car ownership, meant a replanning of traffic flow and transport needs. The caurs were sacrificed and, from September 1962, trundled no more.

Right: In 1955 Renfrew Airport still had over a decade of service to give in its own right. Flying experiments in the region had been conducted from fields in the Moorpark area of Renfrew in 1910 and James Weir and ACH MacLean were flying around farmland, in what was to become Renfrew Airport, during the latter stages of World War I. The War Ministry established an aerodrome at Newmains Farm in 1916 and the 6th Aircraft Park RFC was based at Renfrew the following year. After the war interest in aviation grew and the Scottish Flying Club was formed in 1927. By the outbreak of World War II the club had 11 machines of its own and a membership of 210 pilots, including such notable aviatrices as Winnie Drinkwater, Miss J Waters, Margaret Cunnison and Miss E McDougall. Large crowds were drawn to the flying displays that were a regular feature at the aerodrome. Requisitioned by the Air Ministry in 1939, Renfrew Airport was used, amongst others, by 309 Polish Squadron and in April 1946 became state owned with the establishment of the Civil Aviation Authority. The new terminal that opened on 26 November 1954 was an example of the quite futuristic ideas of designer William Kinninmonth, but the increasing demands of the expanding aviation industry meant that the city needed a more modern and bigger airport. A thanksgiving service for Renfrew's place in history was held in a hangar on 17 April 1966 and Glasgow's new airport opened a fortnight later.

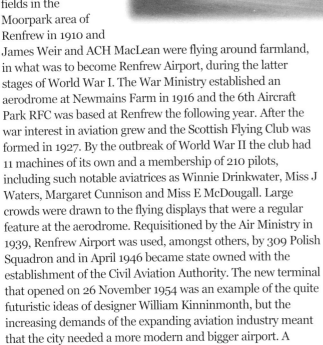

Below: A virtually deserted Renfrew Airport stood under a blue sky in 1955 at a time of great change in air travel, not just for Scots, but for the whole of the western world. Aviation is a child of the 20th century, for it was not until the first decade of the century that Orville and Wilbur Wright first took to the skies at Kitty Hawk in North Carolina. A vast improvement in aeronautical technology was one of the few good things to come out of the 1914-18 war, but, even so, it was not until the 1930s that commercial airliners began to cross continents and oceans. By the time the second world war had concluded, the passenger aeroplane was ready to stake its claim as a major player in the transport industry. The Comet, pioneered by Sir Geoffrey de Haviland, was Britain's first jet airliner, taking to the skies in May 1952 on the BOAC route to Johannesburg. The world was shrinking and before long ordinary people would consider taking to the air in pursuit of some sun on their backs in a foreign clime, rather than being amongst trainloads of holidaymakers descending upon the Clyde coast. Horizons would be widened beyond escape from the oppression of the city with buckets and spades at Largs and Fairlie or taking the paddle steamers to Dunoon and Rothesay. Even Blackpool and the Isle of Man, once seen as great adventures, became mundane. Renfrew Airport's passenger traffic grew from 130,000 per year in 1950 to almost 1,000,000 by the start of the next decade.

Shopping spree

Even in 1928 the junction of Sauchiehall Street and Renfield Street saw plenty of traffic, both on the road and on the pavement. The bobby on point duty directed the vehicles with the flair of an orchestra conductor. Broad, sweeping gestures of his white sleeved arms passed the message to cars and trams to halt or proceed more clearly than any flashing sign on an overhead motorway gantry. The Kirklee tram expected the arbiter of the peace to allow it protected passage and he usually did. In the background other 'caurs', so much a part of Glasgow life, crowded the carriageway. As the years rolled by they became less popular with private motorists who had to wait for them to pass or whose cars skidded on the tracks that became very slippery when wet. Inside McColl's confectionery shop there was scrumptious treacle toffee on sale, just right for rotting more teeth, but such a nice way for them to go! The newspaper vendor, in his flat cap and muffler, was carrying the results of the racing at Ayr. In 1928 he might also have been selling papers that brought news of the successful culmination of the Suffragettes' long struggle when the House of Commons passed the bill giving all women over 21 the vote, at long last. In the same year Amelia Earhart flew the Atlantic and explorer Roald Amundsen died in a plane crash.

Above: The Kelvinside tram, passing James Craig's at 123 Sauchiehall Street, in 1949 carried shoppers who jealously clutched their food coupons and ration books close to their chests. The first few years after the war were difficult times in Britain as we struggled to get back on our feet after six long years of hostilities. The basics were in short supply and rationing of essential items continued until 1954, giving rise to a flourishing black market where spivs could make a living supplying everything from petrol to nylons to those willing to pay over the odds. For the majority of law abiding Glaswegians it was a case of tightening their belts once more and making do with what they could. The artistry of the housewife became all important as she ran up frocks on her old treadle Singer and her knitting needles flew, conjuring up jumpers and mittens from the skein of wool held on her husband's outstretched arms. Even as she did this thoughts turned to how the week's meat ration could be eked out to provide at least one square meal a day for the family. Given that life was tough in those austere years it should come as no surprise to remember that our pleasures often came through entertainment that provided a contrast with everyday life. The escapism provided by the cinema gave us the opportunity to forget, for a few short hours, the problems of the real world outside. The Gaumont, just further west beyond the crossroads with Hope Street, gave the release we needed. It originally opened in 1910 as the Picture House and continued as the Gaumont until 1972 when it was replaced by the Savoy Market.

The sky above Sauchiehall Street in 1929 was festooned with the cables carrying power to the trams that criss crossed the city carrying shoppers and office workers to their destinations. The hard pressed policeman on point duty had to have eyes in the back of his head as he kept the traffic moving safely. Although private motoring was largely confined to the middle classes, the growth in car ownership meant that our roads were becoming more and more unsafe. Fatalities in Britain increased every year during the 20s, rising to nearly 6,000 by the end of the decade. Some 150,000 were injured in accidents and the government started to introduce measures to try to stem the tide. Over the next 10 years traffic lights would appear at busy junctions and crossroads, white lines marking carriageways would be painted on the roads, Percy Shaw's cats' eyes would twinkle in the headlights, driving tests be introduced and pedestrian crossings become commonplace. Education of pedestrians in helping themselves to avoid accidents was instituted and schools undertook the job of instructing children in following the Highway Code and later campaigns, such as 'Stop, look and listen'. The man carrying the sandwich boards was advised to walk the pavements, rather than the streets. At times he would be advising onlookers that 'the end was nigh' or instructing them to 'prepare to meet thy doom'. His message on this day was more economical than spiritual as he advertised the sale of railway lost property that had lain unclaimed. Waterproofs, furs and even a stuffed tiger's head were available at knock down prices.

Above: Charing Cross Mansions is one of the few to have survived from this 1929 view of an area that was one of those extensively remodelled in the 1970s and now striped by the M8 motorway that sweeps along the northern and western edges of the city centre. When people from out of the city speak of tenements they often think of slum dwellings, but the beauty of this curved block gives the lie to that impression. It was originally built in 1891 for the warehousemen Robert Simpson & Sons and is a distinctive landmark, with its ornate clock and carved figures. On the left, the Grand Hotel had seen many famous and titled people pass through its doors. The Prince of Wales stayed here in 1888 before attending the International Exhibition at Kelvingrove, whilst others followed in his wake 50 years later when Bellahouston Park played host to the 1938 Empire Exhibition. On their way there visitors could have called into Harris's tobacconist's next to the Grand. Established in 1881, it was a place where sweet aromas combined with pungent smells. The finest hand rolled Havanas and softly scented pipe tobaccos gave the discerning smoker a feast of sensations that only a true connoisseur could appreciate. On sale, too, were all the associated paraphernalia a smoker might need to enhance his pleasure. There were cigar cutters, ornate cigarette holders, briars, meerschaums and silver cigarette cases that were as much fashion accessories as useful tools.

Inset: The long arm of the avenue that is Sauchiehall Street stretched down to Charing Cross on a sunny day in 1949. Traffic lights helped control the flow of traffic at this busy corner that was one of the most impressive junctions in Glasgow with its group of finely constructed buildings. The lovely cupola on top of Charing Cross Mansions, with its little balcony beneath, nowadays makes a pleasant contrast with the functional, but ugly, sight of the motorway and modern office blocks nearby. When this photograph was taken it seemed as though the war had never really ended, for, even though we celebrated VE and VJ Days four years earlier, the world was still in turmoil.

Mao Tse-tung's Communist troops overran much of China as the British frigate HMS Amethyst made a daring escape down the Yangtse River, the Soviet Union supported the formation of the new East Germany and blockaded Berlin and there were race riots in south Africa and fighting in Kashmir. At home it was still a time of austerity for, although clothing coupons had been abandoned, food and other commodities were in short supply. Consumption of meat and sugar had fallen dramatically and all was not well within the family unit, either. Divorce had increased tenfold since before the war and church leaders bemoaned the breakdown of traditional values.

Below: The Lambhill tram on Renfield Street had just reached the crossroads with St Vincent Street, where it was to cross the path of another of its fellow vehicles carrying passengers ready to shop until they dropped. In 1958 the tills rang merrily as we stocked up with Tide or Omo washing powder, Spangles sweets for the children or Heinz sandwich spread and Marmite for the larder. By this time many of us had even dispensed with larders and cold slabs for we had bought fridges that had once been a luxury, but soon became an integral part of the modern kitchen. Prime Minister Harold Macmillan told us 'We have never had it so good' and he was right. The economy boomed and we entered an era of prosperity never before seen in Britain. We spent more on ourselves than ever before and a new consumer was born around this time - the

teenager. Youngsters developed their own pop culture that was no longer a youthful version of the one adhered to by their parents. They had their own brand of music in rock and roll and their own style of dress with drainpipe trousers or wide, twirling skirts over flouncy petticoats. The advertising moguls recognised a new niche in the market and aimed for the extra target accordingly.

Bottom: The man at the bus stop read his paper patiently as he waited to go home, totally oblivious to the world around him on Renfield Street in 1955. As the street lights came on the Esso sign on the right lit up as well. Even now, those of us who are old enough can remember the advertising slogans of 'The Esso sign means happy motoring, call at the Esso sign' and 'Put a tiger in your tank'. Later, Shell responded with 'Keep going well, keep going Shell' and even used the 60s pop star Georgie Fame's big hit, 'Get Away', as the theme for one campaign. The Morris Traveller, based on the Morris Minor, heading towards the camera, with its timbered coachwork, became a collector's item and is still sought after today, with prices far outstripping the car's real worth. All of life unfolding around the newspaper reader was unimportant to him, for he had found a piece of news that was riveting. Perhaps it was royal gossip that had so entranced him, for in November Princess Margaret called off her proposed marriage with Group Captain Peter Townsend. He was a much decorated fighter pilot and equerry to her late father, George VI, but he was a divorcee and the powers that be had not forgotten the furore over Margaret's uncle, Edward VIII, when his head was turned by the twice divorced Wallis Simpson.

What a lovely couple the elderly pair made as they left the barrows and vans on Ross Street, having bought whatever provisions they could afford on their pensions. Born when Queen Victoria was on the throne, they had lived through the deaths of four monarchs, seen six on the throne, with four being crowned and the abdication of another. Motor cars were introduced to the streets and aeroplanes into the skies. Radio, cinema, gramophones and television were all once newfangled ways to entertain them and wonderful household appliances came along to replace the kitchen range, flat iron, mangle, dolly tub and sweeping brush. What changes they had seen and mostly as man and wife. The institution of marriage that bonded them together was under threat in 1967, as they walked arm in arm in clothing that suited them and ignored the dedicated followers of Carnaby Street fashion. In the swinging 60s free love was the recommendation of those whose first thoughts were of personal pleasure and not responsibility. It seemed to be the case that if you did not experiment with sex, drugs and rock and roll you were out of touch, but how many of those who then went on to burn their bras and embrace flower power can claim to have achieved the happiness and contentment that this couple had for all the world to see?

Above: It was a busy Saturday night in 1955 on the corner of Virginia Street and Argyle Street as shoppers bought the last few items they needed for the weekend from the barrows. Nearby there is now the plaque that marks the fact that Robert Burns once lodged at the Black Bull Inn. Virginia Street is named because of its connection with the tobacco industry that was so important to Glasgow's prosperity 300 years ago. The Tobacco Exchange, with its memories of auctioneers selling off huge quantities of the weed, is situated here, though now called the Virginia Galleries. The site was also the Sugar Exchange, for a while. The little girls on the left wore dresses and little white socks that were the standard uniform of informal attire. If their brothers had been with them, they would have been kitted out in short trousers, knee length socks and a grey or cream shirt. Their fathers wore a jacket to come into town, though many decided that it was all right to leave their ties at home. Mums had begun to dispense with wearing hats, which would have horrified their mothers who believed that it was common to go out of doors bareheaded. Some compromised by wearing a headscarf, just as they had seen Queen Elizabeth do when she was out and about on her estates. If it was fine and dandy for Her Majesty, then it was good enough for us.

Making a living

Above: The Scottish Co-operative Wholesale Society (SCWS) had its headquarters on Morrison Street and was part of the movement that began life in a little grocer's shop on Toad Lane, Rochdale, Lancashire in 1844. Buying and selling goods for its members, the society paid a regular dividend in the form of stamps, known colloquially as the 'divvy'. Before long the movement had spread across Britain, but in 1942 these Co-op workers had more on their minds than savings stamps. They were packing tea rations at the factory in Shieldhall and playing their part in the war effort. With a good eye for hygiene, in their neatly starched mobcaps and overalls, they carefully measured out each allowance that would be permitted to housewives undertaking their shopping foray into Cowlairs Co-op, or which other branch they patronised. The women packing the rations knew that the country was going through a truly bad patch as news from the battlefronts filtered through. Although the censors prevented the full story from reaching the general public, it knew that Singapore fell to the Japanese in February, the Luftwaffe had begun targeting Britain's historic towns in its 'Baedeker' raids and Rommel's panzer divisions had driven back the Allies in North Africa in May.

The woman in the foreground looks thoroughly exhausted as she takes a moment to rest before dealing with another bin full of dirty laundry. It arrived in a never ending succession of trucks, wheeled into the hangar style building like so many wagons in a goods train. She was in the washhouse nicknamed 'Old Steamie', but her thoughts were not about cheery names but of the work that still had to be done before she could take her aching back and reddened hands off home. The large vats boiled the sheets and clothing, giving off clouds of steam that turned into water droplets that made it appear is if she were working in an equatorial climate, so damp and humid was the environment in which she slaved away. Large tongs and paddles were used to manoeuvre the laundry in the boilers and ranks of sinks were provided to help with the hand washing. The Old Steamie had little in the way of the equipment available to the modern industrial laundry or small laundromat. It is easy enough to put a pile of washing into the machine, programme it and leave it while carrying out other jobs, knowing that automation will complete the task without any further help. But these workers knew little of twin tubs and spin dryers because they were part of the technology that lay in the future. Nor was there any such thing as a creche for their offspring. The baby was put in the pram, brought into the washhouse and left there, at the far end of the steamie in those damp conditions, until it was time for mum to knock off work.

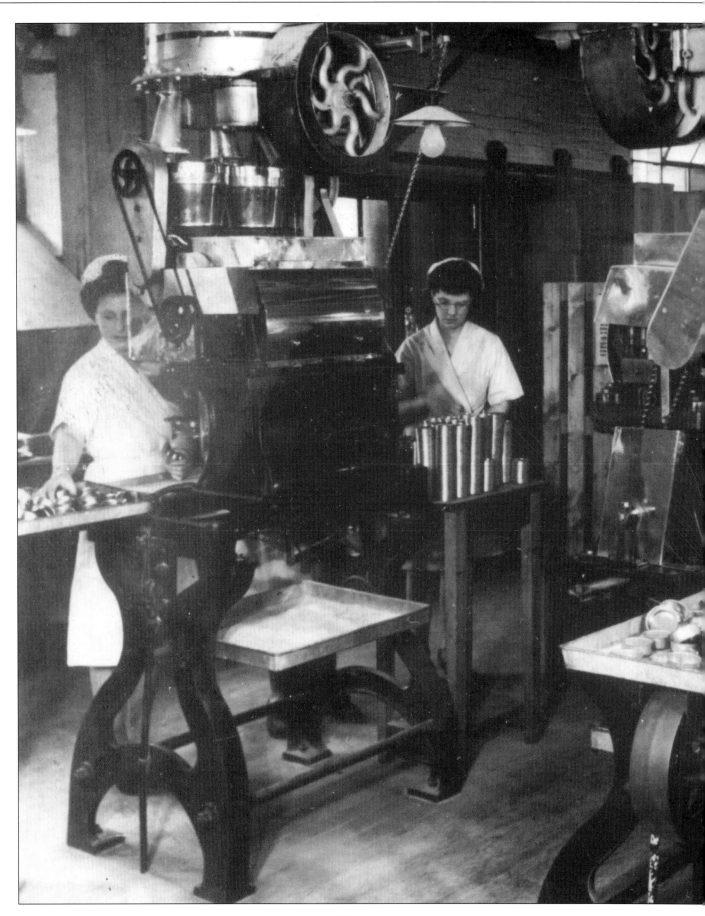

The Co-op workers at Shieldhall packed rations of tea, milk and sugar tablets as they chatted about the events that unfolded across the world in 1942. They had worried that the war was not going well, but in the second half of the year things seemed to be improving. In the summer the Americans routed the Japanese navy at the Battle of Midway and by autumn news came in that Montgomery's Eighth Army had triumphed at El Alamein. The Germans ground to a halt in the winter snows around Stalingrad and the SCWS girls felt as though they could go out on Saturday night and celebrate. They did their hair in the fashion of those charming songstresses, the Andrews Sisters, and put on dresses with hemlines so short that they would have made their fathers blink if they had not been off overseas on active service. Women's hairdos were also influenced by the movie stars they had seen on Hollywood's silver screen, but more practical matters decided their clothing fashions. Material was in short supply, so it was availability and the Board of Trade, not Paris, that set the trends. Utility cloth limited women to some degree, but most had enough needlework skills to be able to adapt the material into more feminine apparel. Then it was off to dance to the 'Boogie-woogie bugle boy' that Patti, LaVerne and Maxene sang of.

Wholesalers, market stallholders, retailers and individual shoppers brought the road to a standstill as the lorries and vans unloaded their produce on the corner of Bell Street and Albion Street for the fruit and vegetable market, near Candleriggs in 1955. Barrows and trolleys were used to take it inside, but there was little chance of clearing it all through the doors in a short time. Anyone wishing to pass along the road had better replan his route, for no one was going to make way until the job was finished. There was too much to do and a large amount of competition to contend with as the traders vied with each other over price and quality. The market was held in the City Halls, where a bazaar first traded in cheese, fruit and vegetables in 1817. In 1841 the halls were built above the bazaar and were used for concerts, dances and lectures, becoming one of Glasgow's most important entertainment and cultural venues. The market ceased to function in 1969, though its structure still occupies part of the site. Candleriggs became a built up street in 1724, ending the work of the candle factories that had operated on the riggs (fields) that were once here. The candle manufacturers had previously been moved to Candleriggs from other parts of the city as they presented a fire hazard.

Above: This trio of Scotstoun shipyard workers had come through the war and were now hoping for a brighter future as the 1950s began. Taking a well earned rest from their toils they hoped that the yards on the Clyde would recapture their old importance. For a while they prospered as the nation rebuilt its war ravaged fleet of merchant shipping, but it was a false dawn of optimism. Far behind them were the heydays that brought Harland & Wolff to Clydeside at the beginning of the 20th century, leading to a situation where 35 per cent of British shipping was built on Clydeside. The 1966 Geddes Report, answering to a Labour government of all things, recommended a winding down of the industry. When the Tories regained power under Edward Heath they forced the liquidation of many once proud companies, leading to sit-ins and demonstrations that were amongst the bitterest ever seen. These Scotstoun men never really considered that the time would come when the hooters calling them to work would fall silent. The industry had provided employment for their fathers and grandfathers before them, but the second half of the century would change their lives completely as they tried to come to terms with the realisation that the country they had fought for no longer needed them, now that the battle had been won.

W hen Faron Young sang 'It's four in the morning' in 1972 he was doing what most country singers do, warbling away about lost love and heartbreak. There was no chance at that very same time before dawn in 1960 to break into any other ditty than 'Yes, we have no bananas' or a chorus of 'Oranges and lemons', because this was the central fruit and vegetable market at Candleriggs. Crowded under its high roof, shopkeepers and stallholders were already wide awake, trying to negotiate the best price for the fruit that would be whisked off for sale to the housewives still in the land of nod, but who

would soon be heading out from home to do the shopping. Spare a thought, as you lie under your duvet on a cold and frosty morning, for the thousands of workers who have been up and about for hours before your toes land on the plush carpet in your centrally heated bedroom. There are food suppliers all over the country arranging that shelves are stocked, fishermen unloading their catch onto the quayside for the auctioneers to sell on, milkmen rattling their gold tops like Benny Hill's 'Ernie', bus drivers and newspaper sellers all part way through their day's work before the rest of the population has as much as risked lifting one eyelid.

Above: The Albion motor works at Scoutstoun, seen in 1955, was part of a motor industry that had yet to face the invasion of cars and commercial vehicles from the rest of Europe and the Far East. The Albion Motor Car Company was founded on 30 December 1899 by, brothers-in-law, Thomas Blackwood Murray and Norman Fulton. The drive and enthusiasm of these two pioneers saw the company flourish and expand rapidly. Adopted in the early stages, the motto 'Sure as the sunrise' was proudly displayed on both radiator and badge right through the model range, signifying robust and reliable vehicles. Life for the company began in a first floor attic of a repair shop on Finnieston Street with just seven employees, yet such was its immediate success that a first export, to Kuala Lumpur, was achieved in 1901. Albion grew rapidly and moved manufacture to Scotstoun in 1903 where its plant occupied over 1,000,000 square feet. It may come as a surprise to learn that in the early days the company was responsible for producing cars, but it was not long before it became more famous for the lorries and buses that bore its proud logo. The company was taken over by Leyland in 1950, but its name survived on vehicles until the 1970s, the last true Albion being built in 1972.

Above right: The women leaving the Twomax factory at 183 Rutherglen Road had just knocked off for the day, their time at the sewing machines done for another twenty-four hours. In the 1960s the clothing industry provided the inspiration for a hugely entertaining television sitcom, 'The Rag Trade'. Starring Peter Jones as the harassed boss, it also featured a strong comic performance each week by Miriam Karlin, playing a feisty shop steward. Any problem that the workforce encountered was greeted by a blow on Miriam's whistle and, with the call 'Everybody out', the girls marched from the cutting room for yet another strike. Although a comedy, 'The Rag Trade' had echoes of real life for industrial action

and an inability to control the unions helped cost the Labour government the general election in 1970. However, these women belonged to the time when few of them had televisions, as the photograph is dated 1956. ITV had only been on the air since September 1955 and the Tories were part way through their 13 years of power. Twomax was established in 1922 by the McClure family and produced fashion goods, especially knitwear, for major stores and the mail order trade. It was later to go into liquidation with a loss of 150 jobs, but a rescue package was put together and, under the guidance of Martin Frost and three other associates, it was revamped with an investment of nearly £2,000,000.

The final journey

No family is immune from death. The only certainties in life are death and taxes and sooner or later we will all need to call upon the services of a funeral director - and when we do we want to have the services of a firm we can trust completely to ensure that events are managed with the utmost tact and professionalism. Often when we need to make such arrangements we are distressed and confused and in need of guidance on what to do. We usually find ourselves asking friends and relatives to make a recommendation of which firm to use, more often than not a firm which has been used by others we know who have found a satisfactory service and who will make such a recommendation. Some of those recommendations go back decades with generations of the same family having used the same funeral director. Such continuity can be important to the bereaved; employing the same firm of Funeral Directors decade after decade creates a family tradition in itself and provides a sense of serenity and completeness in the knowledge that the deceased is being cared for by the same firm which provided a similar service for parents, grandparents and even great grandparents. New firms cannot of course offer such a sense of continuity but one Glasgow firm of funeral directors certainly can.

Almost a hundred years of experience has contributed towards Jonathan Harvey's position as one of the most highly respected firms of funeral directors in the United Kingdom.

Above left: *Founder of the company Jonathan Harvey.*
Below: *The beginning of motorised transportation and its increase was mainly brought on by the Great War, when most horses were shipped overseas to take part in combat.*

That reputation has grown steadily over the years; a reputation enhanced by the care exhibited by four generations of the Harvey family. That dedication is in marked contrast to the ever-growing faceless public concerns and large corporate bodies. Today Jonathan Harvey is still a family business helping the bereaved to cope with the problems and difficulties which face them in their moments of grief.

The Harvey family is proud of its unbroken connection throughout the years with Glasgow and the wider community. During his lifetime Jonathan Harvey was a much respected public figure. He served Glasgow Corporation with distinction for many years while his son Thomas who succeeded him as managing director served as a Justice of the Peace. The company and its reputation grew through the guidance of Thomas and his brother Andrew who were joined by other members of the family who contributed their help to make Jonathan Harvey blossom into the highly respected firm it is today.

The present family concern is controlled by J Andrew Harvey, his wife Linda Harvey and his sister Rosemary Harvey Sinclair who together with their cousin David Harvey are carrying the success of the company into the 21st century. They follow the path of dedication established by the founder and his children. The fourth generation of the family is now represented by Rosemary's daughter Rosalyn Harvey Sinclair a director and the company accountant.

It was Jonathan Harvey who in 1911 formed the company which bears his name. He was indeed a versatile man... originally a motor engineer, he devised the first hackney cab service in Scotland and by 1928 had become a well established Funeral Director.

The first office premises, at 1101 Argyle Street, now serves as Head Office. There are currently six branches in the Glasgow area from which the company is able to offer a comprehensive network of services throughout the central belt of Scotland. The latest evidence of that growth is a new Funeral Home in Drumchapel.

As the oldest original family run concern of its kind in Scotland the company intends to continue its programme of expansion both in terms of service and caring; a community service carried out in the spirit of its founder.

Top: *Jonathan Harvey's first premises.*
Above: *Thomas Harvey (top) and Andrew S Harvey, sons of Jonathan Harvey.*

That spirit of care and service is perhaps best understood by a poem written by Henry Scott Holland (1847-1918) Canon of St Paul's cathedral whose words encapsulate the Harvey's ethos:

Death is nothing at all
I have only slipped away into the next room.
I am I, and you are you.
Whatever we were to each other; that we still are.
Call me by my old familiar name,
speak to me in the easy way which you always used.
Put no difference in your tone,
wear no forced air of solemnity or sorrow.
Laugh as we always laughed at the little jokes we enjoyed together.
Pray, smile, think of me, pray for me.
Let my name be the household word that it always was.
Let it be spoken without effect,
without the trace of a shadow on it.
Life means all that it ever meant.
It is the same as it ever was, there is unbroken continuity.
Why should I be out of mind because I am out of sight?
I am waiting for you,
for an interval somewhere very near, just around the corner.
All is well.

Despite having been in the Funeral Directing profession for so long Jonathan Harvey has however moved with the times and today provides an unsurpassed range of services and resources. The firm's dedication to the highest standards in the profession has made it one of the most respected firms of funeral directors in the United Kingdom.

The same quiet manner pioneered by the original Jonathan Harvey has always been the firm's way, they are still just one family helping other families in their time of need.

From Jonathan Harvey's original Argyle Street premises the firm now co-ordinates services at its individual Funeral Homes in and around Glasgow. In addition to the Sandyford Funeral Home in Argyle Street, Jonathan Harvey also operates The Beeches at Anniesland Road, Victoria Park Funeral Home in Dumbarton Road, The Allander Funeral Home in Drymen Road, Bearsden, Goldenview Funeral Home in Kilbowie Road, Hardgate and the Drumchapel Funeral Home, Kinfauns Drive,

Drumchapel, Glasgow. Together they provide a comprehensive network of support throughout the city and surrounding communities.

Customs are changing and today more and more families use Jonathan Harvey Funeral Homes as a meeting place for friends and relatives prior to the funeral and often for the service itself.

Each of the firm's Funeral Homes is tastefully decorated and includes well appointed rest rooms and a place of worship for both religious and secular services. The homes are never stark and sombre but exude an atmosphere of calm and tranquillity.

The company's fleet of vehicles includes Daimler hearses and limousines, each elegantly finished in Georgian silver and maintained to the highest standards; the company also provides a private ambulance service to nursing homes and hospitals.

This page: *The Jonathan Harvey fleet of vehicles.*

The independent funeral profession has a long and proud history of personal service to local communities. Carrying on the family tradition is a way of life for many independent funeral directors. They are deeply committed to upholding professional standards. Some of the oldest continuously operated businesses in Britain are locally owned family funeral firms.

In all forms of business today however there are large international companies that have made their profits through taking over smaller firms. The funeral profession is no exception. Many businesses have been swallowed up by the giants. The trouble is there usually is no change of name to tell prospective clients the difference. That makes it hard to distinguish between the family owned firm and the conglomerate. Without asking, one might never know if the owners whom one's family has trusted over the years continues to make the decisions which will affect the service they provide when funeral arrangements need to be made.

Large concerns answer to their shareholders. Jonathan Harvey answers to those who choose to use its services. In this locally owned firm there is no pressure from head office to increase profits.

Funeral traditions do vary around the country. Jonathan Harvey knows and appreciates local customs and expectations because it has served the Glasgow community for so many years; the staff and management assigned to a funeral home from a national company may be from another area. Ignorance of local traditions can cause disappointment when expectations are not met.

Not surprisingly then some 60 per cent of funerals throughout the country are arranged by independent funeral directors. Jonathan Harvey is proud to be a member of the National Society of Allied and Independent Funeral Directors, the only professional organisation in the UK exclusively dedicated to serving the local independent family owned funeral director and his or her community.

Through membership of the Society of Allied and Independent Funeral Directors Jonathan Harvey can even assist family in the event of a death occurring far from home.

But wherever and whenever a bereavement occurs the citizens of Glasgow can be sure that the kind of service which only generation upon generation of experience can offer is available to each and every one of them through Jonathan Harvey, Glasgow's most respected firm of funeral directors.

Above: The Jonathan Harvey company premises.
Below left: The Service Room at the Beeches.
Below: Rosemary R Harvey Sinclair (back), (front from left to right) Linda Harvey, J Andrew Harvey, Rosalyn Harvey Sinclair and David J Harvey.

On the road again

People call lorry drivers knights of the road. Kings might be a better description as they thunder along our motorways sitting in the cabs in the massive vehicles high above we commoners. Perhaps carters and hauliers have always been looked up to; certainly we have always needed to move goods from one place to another at first by simple horse power using pack horses to thread their way over the rough tracks which served for roads, then came the canals, their sure but steady progress carrying heavy goods at low cost from one location to another. And then came steam and the age of railways; didn't every small boy, fascinated by the unbelievable power of steam, want to be an engine driver?

But steam did not immediately supplant the canals nor did the canals supplant horses; the changes which we tend to think of as instantaneous happened slowly and horse transport was still common in Britain until the mid 20th century. Only then did the promise made by the internal combustion engine and the improving quality of roads turn back the clock and push both canals and railways aside allowing those who travelled the roads to reclaim their long disputed crown.

The transport and haulage firm of John Smith Transport was founded in 1919 by John Smith the present owners' great grandfather. Today the business is based at 150 Clydeholm Road, in Glasgow, taking its name from its original premises in Whiteinch which the business occupied for over 60 years as well as premises in Ferryden Street.

John Smith was originally a farmer who had come to Glasgow from Ireland; in those early days John Smith ran a farm and sold coal briquettes from a horse and cart - unlike today when the firm's fleet of modern commercial vehicles are used to transport goods such as food, drink, washing powder, building and flooring materials for mainly blue chip household names.

The founder had three sons, William, Thomas and John. It was to be William, who died in the late 1960s, who, after dabbling in farming in Ireland himself as well as haulage in Glasgow who would eventually put the firm on its feet, putting together a veritable herd of horses to run the haulage business. And not only that, William Smith also ran boxing gyms in the city.

William's son, another John Smith and named after his grandfather, was born in 1931 and began working for his father at the age of 12 at the height of the second world war. During the second world war, still using horses and carts, the firm was kept busy locally working for the shipyards moving endless amounts of

Below: *Part of the early John Smith fleet.*

next commission. Horses were used right through the 1940s when they began to be phased out by motor vehicles and quite quickly the firm grew to having 30 vehicles on the road. The first motor lorry John would recall buying was a Bedford though the firm would happily buy Albions, Fords and Scammels.

The switch to motor lorries was hastened in the late 1940s when fire broke out in the firm's garage where a number horses and dogs were killed.

material for Yarrow shipyards, Barclay Curle and Stone Manganese. Encouraged by his father young John would become a well known amateur boxer, and a good one too, fighting all over Scotland.

The younger John Smith began his working life as a trace boy, a young man who waited with a horse at the bottom of a hill until a horse and cart came along that needed some extra horsepower to make it up the slope. The trace boy would hitch his own horse to the wagon until it reached the summit then unhitch from his client and return to the bottom of the hill again to await his

In those late 1940s, following the close of the war, the Labour government nationalised the transport industry. Many medium sized transport firms disappeared overnight to be incorporated into what would become British Road Services. Only very small firms and those with very local businesses escaped the net. Smiths

Top: *Delivery of a Missile test unit for the Falklands War.*
Above: *A John Smith articulated lorry loading up and setting out on the day's delivery.*

being both local and having fortuitously been split into three operating parts would survive as an independent business at a time when many of its competitors would disappear, many to never be heard of again.

It was an opportunity for the business to expand and Smith's lorries soon became an increasingly familiar sight on Britain's roads. The firm's livery was copied from its earlier carts - brown and red chassis and gold leaf writing. Today the lorry livery is white with brown lettering and a prominent 'S' logo acquired in the early 1990s - though red chassis remains as a carryover from the days when the firm's cart wheels were painted in that colour.

The firm became a limited company in the early 1960s when William Smith retired and his son, John, bought what had until then simply been John Smith Transport from him.

Each generation of the Smith family has been involved in the haulage business. The owner of the present business is yet another John Smith; he attended Glasgow's Bearsden Academy before joining his father at the age of 15 in 1970.

At first the younger John worked as a trailer boy, a driver's mate or second man, helping to load and unload vehicles. It was by all accounts very hard work. The working day was seldom less than 12 hours and there were far fewer fork lift trucks abut than there are today to make the job easier.

John recalls that there were very few opportunities for playing pranks and the whole of business seemed far more disciplined than today, though in other respects the work was easier. Drivers who had been on the road all day would congregate in the pub after work to swap tales of life on the road. And life on the road was perhaps happier than today, a lorry driver was alone, a king of the road,the master of his own destiny with no boss looking over his shoulder. Drivers were not kept tabs on by satellite navigation, tachometers and mobile phones; drivers could take their dogs with them for

Above: *Smith's float on Gala day - winning first prize.*

taking goods throughout Britain and western Europe as far as Germany. Over the years the firm has seen diminishing business from traditional industries and has found new clients such as Thomas Tunnock Biscuits, Levers soap powder, Marley building products and Tennant Caledonian brewers. The firm has come a long way from its horse and cart origins and Smith's lorries each travel 100,000 miles a year and are expected to last for ten years, or a million miles, before being replaced at a cost of £60,000 each.

In the new millennium flexibility and accountability are a unique selling point for this business. The current company is wholly owned and run by John Smith and aims to offer not merely flexibility and commitment via their compete knowledge of the transport industry but a first class service from its 16,000 square foot warehouse and 3 acre lorry park.

company if they wished and no-one checked on their working hours or complained if they drove a little faster than the speed limit permitted. Indeed some drivers today recall their youth and will tell you that they could get to their destinations faster in the days before motorways with less traffic on the roads and fewer restrictions on their speed.

But it was still a hard life, made voluntarily even harder by drivers themselves who would rather sleep in their seats than squander their few pounds of 'night out money' on digs. These days of course drivers get what looks like a luxury caravan tacked onto the back of their cabs.

Until 2000 the business was still three separate companies, a legacy of the near nationalisation of the 1940s. On 1st January 2000 the business was formally consolidated as Smith of Whiteinch Ltd under the latest John Smith.

Today the business runs 30 lorries and employs 45 people

And is there to be a fifth generation of Smiths to wear the crown one day? Who can say, but with three sons of his own Mark, Jonathan and Jason the present John Smith would be forgiven for harbouring the hope that one of them might take the steering wheel of the firm founded so long ago by their great great grandfather.

This page *Vehicles from Smith of Whiteinch's current fleet.*

The red carpet treatment

What have you got covering your floors? Fitted carpets in all likelihood. A far cry from the days of our youth. Some of us still recall having nothing over the bare floor except for a rag rug in front of the fireplace. Others will remember lino covering the floorboards and the shock of our young feet hitting the icy floor when we drowsily got out of bed on a cold winter's morning and missed the bedside rug strategically placed to save our tiny toes from freezing.

And for those who did enjoy the luxury of a carpet in the front room there was no such thing as a fitted carpet. Do you remember the large square carpets covering the centre of the room and the floorboards all around painted, stained or varnished on which stood the standard lamps, sideboards and book cases? Do you recall the soft furnishings marooned in the middle of the room with a large rug in front of the fire protecting the larger carpet from stray sparks from the blazing coal fire?

Only in the 1960s did fitted carpets begin to make an appearance in our homes alongside central heating which began to reshape our lives and our living space.

Below: *Decorated to celebrate the Queen's Coronation, Behar's, 11A Bath Street, premises in 1953.*

But back in the 1920s, in the days which are now at the very limit of human memory, where could one buy a really good carpet?

Today Behar Carpets and Flooring specialises in flooring products, from carpets and rugs through to contemporary hard and wooden floors. Products which have been selected through long experience, which represent exceptional value for money for customers and which are supported by a genuine desire by the proprietors to provide the high level of service customers expect.

The business was founded more than 80 years ago by Victor Isaac Behar, an expert Oriental carpet restorer. In the Spring of 1920 Victor, helped by his wife Mildred, opened a small shop at the Charing Cross end of Sauchiehall Street in Glasgow where he sold and repaired Oriental carpets and rugs.

The first known advert for Behar's appeared on the front cover of a programme for the Theatre Royal on Monday 19th September 1921. So successful was this first advert considered to be that further insertions were taken in future programmes - a reproduction from 1923 is shown on these pages. The fact that Behar's was the principal advertiser was already suggestive of the still small firm's aspirations and growing success, its name dwarfing those of lesser advertisers of the time such as Mary London offering 'Marcel Waving' from her salon at Sandyford Place off Sauchiehall Street for 2/6

and the City Gramophone company in Bothwell Street, agents for His Master's Voice offering for sale no fewer than 150 records including those of 'the late Señor Caruso'.

It probably seemed like an auspicious time to start a new business. The first world war, the Great War, the 'war to end war' had drawn to a close at the end of 1918. Millions had died and tens of thousands more civilians had perished in the great flu epidemic which had swept the world in the closing months of the war. Every family, every person, had lost someone who was dear to them and yet there was a spirit of optimism abroad. After four years of constant fear, worry and austerity, people wanted to live again. The 'Roaring Twenties' had arrived and a post war economic boom was underway, unemployment was low and people had money in their pockets.

If Victor Behar had known what lay ahead, he might have had second thoughts about starting up his shop. The post war prosperity of the 1920s would prove to be short-lived and buying luxury carpets would soon begin to feature far less in customers' spending plans. As the 1920s gave way to the 1930s, the great depression threw millions out of work and the stock market crash

Above: Behar's advertising in the 1923 Theatre Royal Programme.

of 1929 left even the previously wealthy counting their pennies. Carpet repairing was now far more likely to feature in Victor's work than sales. And worse was to follow.

During the second world war, business almost ground to a halt with no merchandise, no customers, increasing inflation and serious cash flow problems. With German submarines sinking Allied ships at an alarming rate and the shipping of food, troops and armaments taking a priority, there was little likelihood

Below: *Hand-stitched carpets in Behar's Bath Street premises.*

of space being found for carpets from Asia. Some did arrive however, but not for long. With Japan's entry into the war forming the Triple Alliance with Germany and Italy, invasion of the whole of the Far East, including the taking of the impregnable fortress of Singapore and the threat to British India, Oriental carpets were not high on Winston Churchill's list of priorities. Behar's had much to blame on Messrs Hitler, Mussolini and Hirohito.

However, like tens of thousands of other small businesses, Behar's somehow hung on, inspired by Churchill's speeches and by an indomitable belief that the war would end and that one day business would resume as usual. And of course that faith would ultimately prove to be justified. The first year of peace would see Behar's receive a giant vote of confidence for the future.

In 1946, Victor and his daughter Pearl and son-in-law Sidney Slater, who had joined the business a few years earlier, moved to larger and more central premises in Bath Street. History was not about to repeat itself. Thanks to the new 'Keynesian' economics the slump of the late 1920s and 1930s which had followed the first world war did not reappear in the 1950s and '60s. For once, full employment gave hope and justified confidence in the future. Thousands upon thousands of returned service men now married their sweethearts, in marriages often delayed for years by the war. New homes were being built on an unprecedented scale and those homes needed carpets. Having survived the difficult, desperate years of the 1920s, '30s and '40s Behar's now began to grow.

In 1957, with Caruso having been supplanted by Elvis Presley, Pearl Slater opened and managed the first Edinburgh shop in Castle Street: she would find herself commuting between Glasgow and Edinburgh for the next 35 years. Another stalwart, Ian Murray, joined Behar's in April 1958 and his unstinting support for the company and the Slater family would continue for over forty years.

Pearl and Sidney's son, Martin Slater, joined the family firm in 1963 and after two years training he and his

good friend Leonard Thomson, now tapping their young feet to the sound of the Beatles and the Rolling Stones, were sent to open a branch of Behar's at 31 High Street in Falkirk.

During those years all the family helped in selling goods with Victor and Pearl specialising in buying and Stanley taking care of the financial side of the business.

But the world of commerce never stays still. Sunday trading arrived in Scotland in 1979 and changed the whole nature of carpet retailing; those firms which did not go out of town slowly but surely missed out. Behar's was not going to be one of them, and on Boxing Day 1985 the company opened a new store in Hillington Road, Hillington; and more growth would follow.

Today, directors Martin Slater, David Redman and Bill Bain now preside over a company which has no fewer than 15 branches across the breadth of Scotland. Behar's has become Scotland's largest independent carpet and flooring retailer, competing vigorously with national chains and other independents as it strives for further growth and develops new brands for an evermore discerning public. When Martin's grandfather Victor Behar opened his shop in the 1920s, trams, coal fires and horse drawn transport were still features of the City of Glasgow. In the new millennium a cleaner, brighter, modern city has risen from the old and yet some things have not altered, not least Behar's commitment to a quality service - a business ethos established by Victor Behar at the outset and a fundamental principle which has survived the passage of years to remain the central part of the present company's philosophy down to the present day.

Behar's has moved with the times, long since moving on from the founder's speciality of simply dealing in, and repairing, Oriental rugs. True, the firm still sells such products but over the years the range of items sold has widened to take in every kind of floor covering imaginable - and sold in stores whose size would have made Victor Behar gasp with astonishment had he been told what his small shop in Sauchiehall Street would one day evolve into.

> *Behar's somehow hung on, inspired by Churchill's speeches and by an indomitable belief that the war would end and that one day business would resume as usual*

Thomas Annan - Glasgow's photographic pioneer

In the early 1850s Thomas Annan moved to Glasgow from his home village of Dairsie near Cuper in Fife, to take up a position as an apprentice engraver. One of seven children, Thomas was considered artistic by those who knew him, and he soon became enthusiastic about the new and exciting phenomenon of the day - photography. Together with a friend, a trainee doctor by the name of Berwick, Thomas set up a photography business in 1855. The partnership did not last long, Berwick leaving to pursue his medical career, leaving Thomas Annan to develop the business.

From 1857 the firm operated from the bustling Sauchiehall Street, gaining patronage from the owners of the country houses and mansions around the city, keen to see their property, paintings and family recorded for posterity by the miracle of photography. Many commissions were undertaken for the owners of large properties to have their estates photographed and the prints bound in lavish volumes. Inevitably success led to expansion, and a works was established in Hamilton as early as 1859.

At around this time Thomas lived next door to the sisters of David Livingstone, the famous explorer. As a result of their acquaintance Thomas was able to take what is considered to be the definitive photographic portrait of Livingstone.

Above: *Charles Rennie Mackintosh, who became a friend of James Craig Annan.* *Below:* *Queen Victoria's visit to Loch Katrine.*

Annan's reputation was such that when Queen Victoria visited Loch Katrine, Scotland to open the new water improvement scheme he was chosen to record the event photographically. Another milestone was passed in 1868 when the City of Glasgow Improvement Trust engaged Thomas Annan to make a photographic record of the slum areas before they were demolished. This is one of the first examples of the use of photography as documentary evidence.

Inevitably Thomas's sons, James and John, followed him into the business when they became old enough. James struck up a friendship with the renowned Charles Rennie Mackintosh and took the definitive photograph of him with his distinctive 'floppy bow tie' as well as dozens of contemporary images of his work. The firm were appointed official photographers for the Glasgow Exhibitions of 1888, 1901 and 1911. In 1889 the Royal Warrant was awarded to Thomas Annan and Sons by Queen Victoria. By the turn of the century the Gallery side of the business began to flourish. It became a great social occasion to view a painting by a respected artist in a dimly-lit room, and then to purchase a photo-gravure print of it. Later, it was decided to sell paintings and etchings rather than just prints. Many famous artists held shows in Annan's over the years, but one of the most notable must have been that for L.S Lowry in 1946. All this artistic activity did not mean that photography was neglected by the company. The firm continued to take photographs of Glasgow depicting everything from street scenes and bridges to buildings and tramcars. This collection has found a variety of uses over the years and is still in demand from people undertaking research, or simply seeking an attractive framed image for their home or office.

In more recent times the company was headed by John C. Annan, under whose leadership it moved more into the Art Dealing arena, holding memorable one-man shows and supporting talented, mainly Scottish artists such as Helen M. Turner, James Watt, Hamish MacDonald, Joe Kearney, J.D Henderson, Robert Egginton, Don McNeil, Jean Bell and many others. Sadly, John C. Annan passed away in 1996, but the firm continues to be run as a family concern by his son Douglas Annan, the fifth generation to be involved with the company.

The present-day Gallery at 164 Woodlands Road is only 50 yards away from where the story began. An impressive selection of original paintings can be found at the Gallery, along with the collection of old photographs and a comprehensive restoration and picture framing service. Customers may also view some of the paintings and photographs on the gallery's own website, www.annangallery.co.uk. The company has come a long way since it was established almost a century and a half ago, but the philosophy of providing customers with a friendly and efficient service has remained the same. Thomas Annan would have been proud of that.

Above: *The premises pictured in 1999.*

Mine's a large one

Inevitably, somewhere in this book, there has to be a mention of those who make 'the water of life' - Scotch whisky.

Founded in 1951 by whisky brokers Stanley P Morrison and Mr J Howatt, Morrison Bowmore Distillers Ltd, now a wholly owned subsidiary of Suntory Ltd, is one of the major names in Scotch whisky.

With three malt whisky distilleries situated in the major production areas of Islay, the Highlands and the Lowlands and significant blending, bottling and warehouse facilities the company has established a leading role in the export of Bulk Blend, Vatted Malt and in particular 'Bottled in Scotland' blends and Single Malts.

The success of Morrison Bowmore is based upon the maintenance of traditional values coupled with innovation in the market place.

Bowmore Distillery on the inner Hebridean Island of Islay was first legalised in 1779 and is one of the oldest distilleries in Scotland. Situated on the shores of Loch Indaal it was acquired by the company in 1963 and is one of only five malt whisky distilleries in Scotland which still have traditional floor maltings.

What was then still Stanley P Morrison Ltd whisky brokers moved in to distilling at a time when many disused distilleries were being decommissioned. The expansion in trade in the

1960s however resulted in malt whisky output rising from 65 million litres of pure alcohol (LPA) to 1214 million LPA by 1968.

When Morrisons made its purchase it was the first of a series of steps taking it to the forefront of the small independents in the whisky industry. The Roseburn Bonding company was soon acquired to extend storage and create valuable blending facilities in Glasgow and this was soon followed by the Tannochside Bonding Company in 1965. New warehousing was built to hold 5 million gallons (22.7 million litres) of spirit. The company's distilling interests were soon extended further by the acquisition of the Glengarioch distillery near Old Meldrum.

Glen Garioch distillery, purchased by the company in 1970, was established in 1797 in the village of Old Meldrum near Aberdeen and produces the company's Highland malt. Fourteen years later yet a third distillery had been added to the fold.

Top: *Bowmore Distillery situated on the shores of Loch Indaal on the inner Hebridean Island of Islay.*
Right: *Auchentoshan Distillery in Dalmuir.*

of the Old Kilpatrick hills overlooking the river Clyde the distillery has witnessed many historic sights over its long existence. From the sailing ships loaded with both legal and illegal whisky leaving the Clyde destined for the four corners of the world to the vast cargoes of spices, tobacco, cotton and wine arriving in Scotland that made Glasgow such a prosperous trading city. And the distillery has watched the birth of the huge Clyde-built ships such as the Queen Mary and Queen Elizabeth I & II, the hallmark of shipbuilding and engineering excellence.

In 1995 the 'International Wine and Spirit Competition' declared Morrison Bowmore Distillers 'Distiller of the Year; the first name to go on the new trophy and awarded for the 'consistency and excellence in distilling, packaging and branding for its Bowmore and Auchentoshan brands'.

In each of the following three successive years the company also received the Queen's Award for Export Achievement in recognition of its outstanding sales abroad.

And the superb quality of those exports continued to be recognised with the company being declared International Distiller of the Year in 2000 in the International Spirits Challenge - and Distiller of the Year in both 2000 and 2001 in the San Francisco World Spirits competition.

Auchentoshan is a rare delight, besides being one of the few Lowland single malt distilleries still in production it is unique in that the whisky is triple distilled rather than the usual double distillation. The distillery was bought by Morrison Bowmore in 1984 and has been completely refurbished in recent years.

Although the traditions of distilling are as important today as they ever were at Morrison Bowmore Distillers Limited this is a company with vision and that ambition is still growing. The company has the incentives and the ability to be innovative, to move quickly and yet to continue to provide the highest level of personal service within the Scotch Whisky industry.

The Auchentoshan distillery was established in 1823 and since then has had just six careful owners each of whom has handed down its unique production process. From the foot

Top left: The unique triple distillation method at Auchentoshan Distillery. ***Above left:*** *The Tun room at Auchentoshan Distillery.*
Below left: *Auchentoshan Distillery, Dalmuir.* ***Below:*** *Auchentoshan Lowland Single Malt Whisky.*

Safety first - 50 years on

The story of Scotland's premier protective clothing supplier goes back at least as far as 1924 when the business was then owned by John Corston Sinclair, a wireless, electrical and rubber merchant. What was then the firm of J Corston Sinclair & Co operated from the centre of Glasgow at 25 Wellington Street, just a few yards from the old Alhambra Theatre.

In 1949 however, Robert Forrest McIlwham and Ben Gough formed a partnership to buy the business from its founder and decided to concentrate on the rubber merchant side of the business. Capital was scraped together to buy the business and this was successfully achieved with assistance from Sophie, Robert's wife. Robert's brother James joined the firm in the early 1960s as bookkeeper and Robert and Sophie's son Sandy joined the company after his education at Hutchesons' Grammar School in 1960. This was the start of the family business.

It was difficult building a business from scratch but Robert ran the company in an admirable style, quickly gaining the respect of suppliers and customers. Most of the customers at that time were in the centre of Glasgow, so goods were very often delivered by hand or with a barrow. This was a common delivery method in these days, with the increase in traffic in an already overcrowded city. The storeroom and office was 'one stair up' so when carriers dropped off deliveries these had to be manually handled up the stairs. This certainly kept young Sandy fit as the only storeman. The business employed 5 people in the 1960s.

As a rubber merchant the business supplied hose, sheeting, gaskets and plumbers sundries and at one time the firm also supplied all the Scottish Golf Club manufacturers with a moulded rubber undergrip over which a leather grip was wound, supplying such famous names as Wilson, Slazenger, Dunlop, Auchterlonie and John Letters.

As time went on the product range increased to include oilskins and wellington boots and as safety legislation kicked in, head to toe protection was added leading the firm to adopt the business banner of 'Scotland's Protective Clothing Centre'. Well before then however, in the late 1960s, the firm had moved from the busy city centre to the developing industrial area of East Kilbride a fast growing area on the outskirts of Glasgow. This was the catalyst for the further success of the business, which was going from strength to strength and building a strong reputation in the area of personal protective clothing.

Local staff were employed mostly from local schools and trained in the Corston Sinclair way of working. So successful was this, that even now certain key members of staff are still with the business after all these years.

Due to the increase in business the small factory in East Kilbride was soon doubled in size with the takeover of the unit next door. As business grew so did staff members and more space was required for increased stockholding so with assistance from the East Kilbride Development Corporation a larger unit within the same industrial estate of College Milton, was obtained. Sadly, before this move, Robert died in 1972.

Above left: *Robert Forrest McIlwham, founder of the company.* **Above right:** *A Corston Sinclair quote from 1924.* **Right:** *The first premises in Wellington Street.*

James had died earlier and Ben Gough had retired, leaving Sandy to run the business, which had now been formed into a limited company, Corston Sinclair Limited. Sandy brought in Eric Schofield to look after the financial side of the business and later Bob Allan to takeover the sales side and enable Sandy to concentrate on the management of the business.

Once again the business was dealt a sad blow when Bob Allan died after a long illness so Sandy turned this time to promote Derek Schofield, who had been in the business since he left school, worked in the warehouse, Sales Office, Sales Representative and latterly Sales Manager, to the post of Sales Director. Business was still developing at a growing rate and in 1977 the decision was made to find a factory, which would allow for future expansion. So Corston Sinclair bought the now empty Bowater Scott factory in Glenburn Road, East Kilbride. This is their present factory which offers good vehicle access, easy parking, a large Trade Shop and also houses the manufacturing and embroidery unit.

The manufacturing side of the business was set up in 1973 to manufacture special garments. Initially run by Sandy under the name RFM Workwear, RFM being his fathers initials (Robert Forrest McIlwham). This unit made exclusively for Corston Sinclair, mainly making ladies coveralls and having the facility for sewing on name badges and company logos. The manufacturing unit is now under the Corston Sinclair wing and has recently invested in an embroidery machine, which is proving a real success story due to the growth of Corporate Workwear and Clothing. 'RFM' still remains the company brand name and the manufacturing unit is now under the watchful eye of Derek Schofield.

Sandy McIlwham, now Managing Director, would eventually also have two of his sons in the business, Zander joined in 1985 and is now Area Sales Representative; Gordon joined a

short time later as Warehouse Manager but at present is enjoying a successful professional rugby career being capped a dozen times for Scotland, although still keeping a close interest in the Company.

Sandy and Zander share a keen interest in the ancient Scottish Sport of Curling and an opportunity presented itself to supply curling equipment to sports shops and ice rinks throughout the UK and Europe. That proved a very interesting diversification for the company, which is now the sole UK Supplier for curling shoes, brushes, clothing and accessories. A small niche market, which has nothing to do with protective clothing.

Today the firm of Corston Sinclair Limited is Scotland's leading independent suppliers of protective safety clothing and workwear which it supplies to the food, fish, electronics and engineering industries as well as local authorities, utilities and agriculture throughout Scotland.

As well as having three full-time area sales representatives on the road and an excellent inside sales staff the company also has a large trade shop to service its many local customers. A family firm, after all these years, the company prides itself on offering a genuinely personal service with its staff of 22, most of whom have been with the firm for many years. Sophie McIlwham, despite being in her mid eighties, still keeps a close eye on her investment by remaining a non-executive director.

Keeping abreast of new development is always on the agenda at management meetings and of course the age of e-commerce is now upon us. Corston Sinclair have their own website now at www. corstonsinclair.com.

A far cry from pushing a barrow up Wellington Street!

Above: An example of protective clothing supplied by the company. Left: Sandy McIlwham, Managing Director of Corston Sinclair Ltd. Far left: The Corston Sinclair Ltd company premises, Glenburn Road, East Kilbride.

Spowart labels...stuck on success

Anyone familiar with the ancient art of supermarket shopping will know that the exercise is made so much easier because we can instantly recognise our favourite products by the labels on the tins and packets. They become our friends and any slight change in their appearance catches our attention.

We take these so much for granted that we fail to appreciate the fact that many people's working lives are taken up in designing and printing them. The story of WG Spowart spans the history of this industry from its earliest days right up to the present time. It is a fascinating history, especially as succeeding generations of the same family have taken up the new challenges encountered on the way.

The story begins in 1862 when William Guild Spowart and George W Haviland formed a partnership as 'Chromolithographers and Stationers' based at 24 Howard Street, Glasgow. Thirty four years later this partnership was dissolved when William Spowart bought out his partner's share for £300. William G Spowart took on his son, William Inglis Spowart (who was 26 at the time) and they moved the business to 99 Maxwell Street, Glasgow where they traded successfully, gradually increasing their turnover.

In those early days printing was an extremely labour intensive process. Stones, engraved by artists were used as printing plates. Later zinc or aluminium plates were used. This is a far cry from the computer to plate processes which are used today or the latest digital technology which is in widespread use, and which can deliver the amazing volume of over 40 million labels printed by Spowarts every week.

Such was their success that the father took the son into partnership in 1906. The firm's capital at that time was £2015/17/5d. Wages for both partners were fixed at £3 per week on

Top left: *Founder, William Guild Spowart.*
Above: *A letter from William G Spowart with an offer of £318 17/10d to buy out the partnership in 1896.*
Below: *Working on the press in the 1940s.*

the condition that, William I (son) 'shall devote his whole time and attention to the business' and Wm G (father) 'be bound to devote only such time and attention thereto as he shall find convenient or think advisable'. At that time an association with the firm of Wm H Jack was commenced who provided audit and accountancy services, a tradition which continues to this day.

Wm G died in 1912 after 50 years in the printing business leaving the firm in the hands of his son, then aged 32 years. The firm moved during the course of the year to newer premises in 136 George Street where it remained until 1928 when a mutually advantageous arrangement of rent sharing with Whitbread Brewers at 520 Garscube Road, Maryhill, Glasgow was concluded. One further move, to its present premises in Queenslie on the east side of the city, took place in 1948.

The first world war had an enormous impact on Spowart's business, in common with all others. Perhaps the most significant was the lack of skilled workers and machinery which occurred at the time. A letter dated 1919 from a leading print engineering company from Fred Furnival of Furnival & Co. Stockport apologises for the lateness of delivering a new machine due to the shortage of necessary materials. A second-hand (reconditioned) machine was delivered instead.

Up to this time the business was very much a family concern as business was small enough for all the main management functions to be undertaken by a single person. This is of course a situation which had to change as the company grew and the business environment became more complex. The main focus of the firm was originally the printing of general stationery items, but around the 1930s the company diversified into printing paper wrappers for biscuit tins. This was to become the mainstay of the business for many years until expansion into the food and drink business during the 1960s provided the basis for the business as it is today.

The third William Spowart joined the business in 1930, this time William G. He had trained as an accountant and his brief was to build up a portfolio of clients south of the border. This entailed considerable absences from home as, at the time, roads were bad and other means of transport extremely slow. He was able to secure the custom of such well-known named in the biscuit industry as Fox's, Beatties, Elkes's, Westons, Wrights and Burton's. His younger brother Dan joined the firm soon afterwards.

Top: A Crabtree two-colour press in the 1960s.
Above: William I Spowart (left) and William G Spowart.

In 1939 the business was converted to a private limited company. WI Spowart, who had been the sole partner since 1912 sold it to his two sons, Wm G and Daniel E K Spowart and their four sisters, Nan, Helen, Irene and Louise for £15,300 and was incorporated that year as WG Spowart Ltd with Wm I as Chairman, Wm G as company secretary and Dan in charge of sales.

Throughout the war years the company traded for itself in the biscuit and label industry and also undertook work for the war effort. In 1942 a new rotary press which had been purchased for £2,200 was commandeered by the government for Ministry of defence work and re-purchased at a somewhat lower figure. The business, like so many, struggled to survive during the war years with materials difficult to come by, spare parts for machinery largely unavailable and a huge shortage of skilled men and women to do the work. Those who had been around during the first word war found this a familiar scenario.

In 1942 Wm I died at the age of 72 and William G became Chairman. His brother Dan became Director responsible for sales before he was called up to serve in the RAF. The business continued to be run during the day by Wm G, while at night he served as a volunteer on the Clyde patrol for the Royal Navy. In spite of all these problems the company continued to trade, supplying packaging for the food industry and even managed to show a modest profit throughout these difficult war years. The move to Queenslie took place in 1948, and Spowart's had found a permanent home on a new industrial site. It was a new purpose-built single level factory and offered ideal accommodation for the firm. They installed the first Roland press from Germany in Scotland during 1952 at a then considerable price of £8,500. This marked a new era in the printing trade. Spowarts recognised with some regret that Germany was now deposing the UK at the forefront of printing technology, and Roland today remain alongside Heidelberg as the leaders in printing technology throughout the world. The Spowarts family had been supporters of the major British companies such as Furnival, George Mann and Crabtree throughout the first half of the century, but each, in turn, went to the wall or was taken over because of lack of investment. Spowart's took on board the message - and have, ever since, always invested as heavily as possible to remain at the sharp end of technological developments, a practice which has undoubtedly contributed much to their present day success.

The stated aim of the company is to provide quality printed products designed to give total customer satisfaction; right first time, every time. Spowarts offer a varnishing service to further enhance or protect printed labels. A varnish can be in-line or off-line, depending upon the number of colours and design of the label in either a high gloss or matt finish using the latest drying technology of ultraviolet or infrared.

Above: Early labels printed by Spowart's.
Below right: An old Spowart platemaking machine. *Below:* An original Heidelberg Platen press, circa 1920.

comedy pantomime duo, Francie and Josie. Each year the starlet would visit the company and would often be give a tour of the works.

By now the fourth generation Wm Spowart was ready to join the firm. This happened in 1977 after Wm I had graduated from printing college and had completed a year's training in Germany.

This was an exciting time for the printing industry with many new technologies and processes becoming available. In 1978 the firm took delivery of its first four-colour press and only four years later installed a six-colour press, the first of its kind in the UK.

Throughout the next 20 years or so the company continued its investment strategy in new machines. Famous names which helped to cement the foundation for the current business includes AG Barr, Scottish Animal Products of Barrhead (which subsequently became Dalgety Spillers), Wilsons of Kilwinning (which became Hillsdown Holdings) and J&P Coats the famous thread makers of Paisley.

A popular Spowart tradition is the regular company night out. In the 1960s and 1970s many of these were enjoyed at the Pavilion Theatre with every Glaswegian's favourite

New generations come onto the scene and older ones bow out. William G Spowart died in 1988 on the eve of his 82nd birthday. He had enjoyed robust health well into his 70s and maintained his interest and involvement in the company as chairman until his death. He had worked for the firm for 58 years, 46 as Chairman and Managing Director.

Top: Barrs Lemonade label being cut to shape in the 1950s. *This operation is now fully automated.*
Above left: *Mr Spowart shows the actress Eunice Gayson around the factory at Queenslie in 1953.*

During the 1990s, the company saw continued investment and market share growth under the chairmanship of William I Spowart, great grandson of the founder. Several million pounds were invested during this period to consolidate WG Spowart Ltd as one of the most forward-thinking companies in the label industry.

The new century saw the firm established as the second biggest independent label producer in the UK, supplying over 40 million labels per week throughout the UK and Europe for all major supermarket groups and household names. It enjoys a well-earned reputation as a trusted and well-established company, but never rests on its laurels, continually considering new trends and acquiring new technology and skills as they develop.

One of its proudest associations is with another of Glasgow's well established but somewhat more famous names, AG Barr, for whom Spowarts has supplied labels since the early 20th century and it is a great source of satisfaction that the two companies continue to trade successfully together.

WG Spowart Ltd now employ over 100 people, who work in three shifts around the clock and is proud of the many employees who have worked for them for over 25 years, of whom there are now literally dozens. One gentleman clocked up a grand total of 51 years before he retired, aged 65. The combination of experience, latest technology and the continued commitment of the Glasgow workforce and management will ensure the company will survive until the fifth generation of Spowarts is ready to give its own input to the family firm.

Spowarts have the in-house capability to receive and handle label designs created in any of the mainstream software packages. Designs can be received on disc, through PDF exchange or through their ISDN link. Advice on design and layout can be given at this early stage to ensure label design integrity is maintained and is practical for production purposes. They work in close liaison with their retained origination house to ensure high quality of all digital designs - from proof - to plate - to press.

One facility which sets Spowarts apart from its competitors is their ability to print on many substrates, so labels can be produced from plastic, metallised and holoprism papers as well as metallised plastics which is a material particularly favoured by the household and fabric conditioner industries.

In 1994 the company was one of the first in the printing industry to be awarded the International Quality Standard ISO 9002 and in 1996 won an international Export Award sponsored by Scottish Enterprise, culminating in the winning of the coveted 'Label Printer of the Year' award in 1998. William Spowart acknowledged at the awards ceremony in London that this was particularly welcome as it was an award which customers had voted for, and was a tribute to the

Top: *William I Spowart standing alongside a new press.*
Above: *Spowart's state-of-the-art guillotine.*

commitment everyone had shown in bringing Spowarts to the forefront of the British printing Industry. Quality is recognised by everyone in the firm as being their responsibility, and the quality control department is manned twenty-four hours a day just like the presses themselves. Spowart's computer systems drive the flow of work from the design through to completion and to sustain quality and accuracy, all production areas are environmentally controlled.

As well as being firmly established in the UK, the company has growing markets in Ireland, France, Italy, Netherlands and the Benelux countries.

Spowarts will continue the family tradition of continual measured expansion, purchasing new technology where appropriate, and continuing their commitment to training and developing their workforce. In the opening year of the new

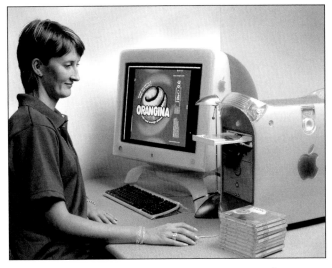

century, Spowart's investment programme amounted to over £2 million, £1.5 million of that went on a new printing press.

Everything in the Spowart garden is rosy, but they have one grievance. After nearly 140 years people still insist on pronouncing their name wrongly! For those not in the know, the correct pronunciation rhymes with 'cow' not 'oh'.

Above: *Using the latest technology in label design.*
Left: *A selection of labels designed and printed by Spowart's.*
Bottom: *A staff photograph on the new press, June 2001.*

Helping make Glasgow 'miles better'

As Christmas 1963 approached a young Chartered Surveyor decided to decline the offer of a partnership in a leading city firm and set up business on his own account.

Despite having the responsibility of a wife and a young family Colin Robertson put up his name plate at 144 St Vincent Street and hoped that his confidence would not prove ill founded.

The building which provided him with his first tiny seventh floor office was the famous Hatrack building, the creation in 1899 of leading architect James Salmon II, and a fine example of the late Victorian architecture for which Glasgow is so rightly renowned.

The early 1960s were not however vintage years for the city: years of neglect caused by various factors including Rent Restrictions Acts and the second world war had left a legacy of crumbling tenement buildings, the worst of which were being swept away and replaced with unimaginative concrete boxes, largely devoid of any architectural merit or suitability for their occupants.

The redevelopment of outmoded and substandard commercial and residential property which was then being carried out under the control of the Glasgow Corporation was depressing, but the private developments of the time were often equally lacklustre. A large majority of private house building was controlled by one or two house builders who had the foresight to secure most of the available land suitable for development. A lack of competition also meant lack of incentive to produce imaginative house design and neighbourhood layouts.

The transformation of the city to what it has become today is then all the more remarkable considering the speed with which it would be achieved.

The catalyst for action was the unlikely but inspired partnership between the national Conservative government and Glasgow's Labour administration which emerged in the late 1970s.

This provided central funding which enabled generous Improvement Grants to be given to underwrite major refurbishment of the city's tenement properties. Within a few years the concept took off and within a decade re-roofed and stone-cleaned buildings with modern windows and internal services were the rule rather than the exception. Tenement backcourts which had

Colin Robertson Graham & Partners combined skills cover every aspect of your property.

CRGP
Colin Robertson Graham & Partners

Above left: *Founder, Colin Robertson.* **Above:** *CRGP's Award winning innovation advertisement.* **Left:** *The Victorian Hatrack building.* **Below:** *Guy Robertson (agent) and James Graham (partner) pictured in front of buses carrying CRGP advertising.*

been allowed to deteriorate to slum standards were transformed into areas once more suitable for family use.

By the mid 1970s the young single practitioner who had set out on his own a decade earlier had joined forces with his quantity surveyor friend James Graham and relocated to a more suitable office in the leafy suburb of Bearsden. This provided more spacious and flexible premises with car parking facilities and good public transport links as well as offering an excellent local pool of both professional and secretarial staff. Here they pulled together a team of professionally qualified partners and staff who collectively brought the skills of architecture, quantity surveying, building surveying, valuation and estate agency into one comprehensive property service. At this stage of the practice's growth the firm's name had become Colin Robertson Graham & Partners reflecting the expansion of the partnership.

CRGP, as the firm later became known, was therefore well prepared to undertake the multi-discipline professional property services required by the local authority and housing associations which were responsible for implementing the Improvement Grant schemes.

The effect of the visible improvement in the city's appearance soon translated into a growing confidence in its citizens who began the transition from being disgruntled owners and tenants of decaying properties to proud property owners who extolled the benefits of Glasgow and helped to revitalise its commercial and leisure activities.

In parallel with that transformation CRGP also grew in stature and confidence, and throughout the 1980s and early 90s expanded its services throughout the greater West of Scotland area opening offices in Ayr, Hamilton, Helensburgh, Paisley and Saltcoats in addition to its bases in Glasgow and Bearsden.

The marrying of the skills of the architect, quantity surveyor and project manager, under one roof, led to the successful development of a truly multi-disciplinary team with the CRGP architects and surveyors division becoming one of

the principal players engaged in saving much of Glasgow's Victorian tenement heritage.

Due to years of neglect combined with structural problems one building on the Gallowgate, Dovehill Court, was in danger of being demolished, many of the nearby houses having been vacated. However, with the assistance of the City Council and a privately funded development company, the building was fully refurbished by CRGP and the flats reoccupied.

Demographic changes in the city's population were mainly brought about by the clearance of entire areas of sub-standard tenement buildings. Many of the old occupants were given new accommodation in the outlying areas of Drumchapel in the west, Castlemilk in the south and Easterhouse in the east, together with the new towns of Cumbernauld and East Kilbride.

This resulted in several Victorian school buildings becoming surplus to educational requirements, but fortunately many of those fine buildings were saved and converted to residential use.

Stewartville Primary School for example, a large and imposing building famed for once accommodating the young Billy Connolly, made a significant contribution to the local streetscape. The CRGP

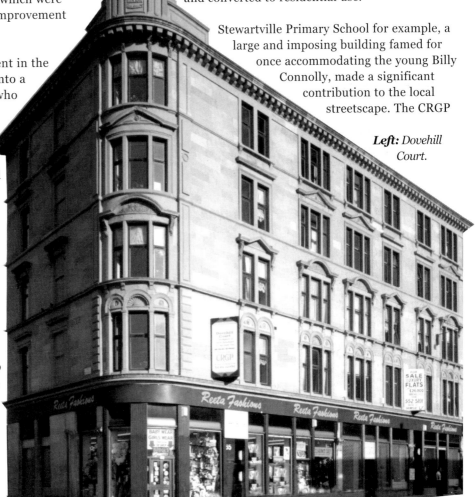

Left: *Dovehill Court.*

team of architects and surveyors, together with a public-private consortium, developed and managed a scheme which saw the building happily converted to residential use.

The experience gained by the CRGP architects and surveyors division in the refurbishment of Victorian tenements and schools allowed the team to undertake more unusual restoration work, a fine example of which is the former corn mill on the banks of the River Kelvin at Kelvinhaugh.

This ancient building was taken back to its four walls and, again with public-private funding, was successfully converted into attractive flats for owner occupation.

In 1984 with over 100 partners, professional assistants and secretarial support staff to accommodate, and with an increasing workload coming from city sources, the partnership purchased the former Scots Guards' club premises at 12 Lynedoch Place in the Park area which became CRGP's new Head Office.

Refurbishment work continued to form a large proportion of the firm's activities but this did not affect parallel growth in the fields of residential surveys, valuations, general practice and commercial work.

The general practice division of the firm became one of the principal surveyors and valuers appointed to undertake mortgage valuations for the country's leading banks and building societies at the same time gaining a well deserved reputation for providing sound advice to prospective home buyers and small businesses.

Above: Stewartville Primary School converted by CRGP for residential use. **Right:** *Bishopmill, converted into luxury flats for owner occupation.*

In the early 1980s whilst giving priority to providing independent professional advice to public bodies, financial institutions and private individuals, the partnership also undertook two developments on its own account, each of which proved a considerable challenge involving all the professional skills at its disposal.

The first development involved the purchase of land in the Algarve where planning permission was obtained for three substantial villas. Upon completion of the first villa, which was built in the local style by a Portuguese builder, it was decided to defer building the other two villas and to retain the first for the use of the partners, staff and their family and friends.

Quite unexpectedly this led to the firm becoming consultants to many existing clients from the Glasgow area who wanted to develop or acquire houses in the Algarve themselves but were uncertain of the procedures to be followed and were wary of foreign builders and solicitors.

Another development privately funded by the CRGP partners was the refurbishment of Westerton of Mugdock, a former mansion house occupying a fine elevated site overlooking Glasgow from above the Milngavie waterworks.

The building had been used as a children's home and required extensive restoration work and alteration to provide eight homes and four detached cottage buildings, each with its own individual character.

Although not major property developments both of these projects involved every single professional

discipline of the partners. The fact that almost all of the properties created are still occupied by the original purchasers would be a source of considerable pride and satisfaction to all concerned with their creation.

In 1995 the problem again arose of outgrowing the existing office accommodation and this, together with the increasing parking congestion at the Lynedoch Place office in the Park area, led the partners to seek a radical solution.

The former six storey printworks and warehouse built in the late 19th century in Herbert Street off North Woodside Road, Kelvinbridge had laid empty for some years; it was completely neglected and was deteriorating rapidly.

With commendable foresight the CRGP partners devised a scheme for the complete renovation and adaptation of the Herbert Street building to provide over 18,000 square feet of attractive modern office accommodation around a central atrium with open galleries providing access at each floor.

At this point two significant developments took place. Firstly Brunton Miller, the firm of city solicitors with whom the CRGP partnership had maintained close relations ever since Colin Robertson and senior solicitor Douglas Dalgleish had first met over 30 years earlier, indicated that they too needed new accommodation and wanted to move from the crowded city centre.

Above left: *12 Lynedoch Place, former home to the Scots Guard club, purchased in 1984 by CRGP to become their Head Office.*
Above right: *Herbert House before renovation.* ***Left:*** *The central Atrium in Herbert House.*

from the complete range of disciplines available from partners and staff.

Ever since its move to Lynedoch Place CRGP has had an affinity with the Park area of Glasgow and the early years of the 21st century would see the firm working on upgrading and conversion projects at Woodlands Terrace and Park Circus.

In these cases CRGP Robertson has been advising on marketing and sales issues with CRGP Architects and Surveyors undertaking project management responsibilities.

The Park area was originally developed in the mid 19th century with grand town houses for the city's merchant princes and professional classes. In the 1960s and 70s the houses became too large for individual family use and were gradually converted to offices.

Then in the last few years of the 20th century, following the increasing demand for residential accommodation within convenient distance of the city centre, the trend was reversed. Many of the buildings were now restored to their former use, albeit with each original unit now providing several self contained flats, retaining where possible the original

Secondly the Glasgow Development Agency and the Dunbar Bank were sufficiently impressed with the proposals for the new Herbert House and the quality of the firms involved that they agreed to provide sufficient financial support to enable CRGP to carry out the development.

The completed building would be a fine testimony to the enterprise of the CRGP partners who brought it to fruition, and it is now greatly enjoyed by those who work there and is admired by visiting clients.

Moving forward into the new millennium, the what are now two inter-related CRGP partnerships continue to provide integrated professional advice on virtually all aspects of property to a wide range of clients.

From the simple valuation of a small house to the planning and management of extensive residential, commercial and leisure developments, the necessary expertise is available

Above: *Herbert House after renovation.*
Below: *An Aerial view of Woodlands Terrace and Park Circus upgraded by CRGP.*

ornate stonework, plasterwork, stained glass, hardwood floors and other period features.

From the earliest days of the partnership the principals have recognised the importance of people in their organisation and equally the importance of training .

It was not surprising therefore that the CRGP Robertson partnership was the first general practice firm of chartered surveyors in Scotland to be accredited under the British Standards ISO 9000 for Quality Assurance, and that, shortly thereafter CRGP Architects and Surveyors was similarly accredited. CRGP Architects and Surveyors also gained the prestigious 'Investors in People' award.

Innovation and progress have always been at the core of the CRGP policy and in 1998 Colin Robertson, and his partner and colleague for more than 30 years, George S Watt, were instrumental in forming Allied Surveyors Scotland Plc.

This brought together a number of highly regarded firms of chartered surveyors who between them had 34 offices covering all areas of Scotland. They would be linked with a sister organisation, Allied Surveyors Plc, which had over 100 offices in England, Wales and Northern Ireland. The Allied

Surveyors organisation would be the largest firm of its type in the United Kingdom.

As founder members of that alliance which provides 'National Coverage and Local Knowledge' CRGP Robertson had taken another innovative step forward for both its own professional satisfaction and for the benefit of its clients.

CRGP Architects & Surveyors, and its offshoot CRGP Management Services, have also extended their fields of expertise to include the specialised areas of healthcare, leisure, public utilities and defence estates and are now increasingly working throughout the whole of the UK.

Colin Robertson is understandably proud to have been the source of these firms whose reputations are based upon the testimony of thousands of satisfied clients; the present partners intend to ensure that their well earned reputation is carried forward and enhanced in the years ahead.

Above: *CRGP accredited under the British Standards ISO 9000 for Quality Assurance.* ***Below:*** *Delegates to Scottish Conference of Allied Surveyors.*

Children taking part in the celebrations to commemorate Queen Elizabeth II's coronation on 2 June 1953.

Acknowledgments

The publishers would like to thank
Douglas Annan at the Annan Gallery
The staff at the local studies section of the Mitchell Library

Thanks are also due to
Andrew Mitchell who penned the editorial text
and Steve Ainsworth for his copywriting skills